I AM THE LORD YOUR HEALER

ROANNA BALETA

I AM THE LORD YOUR HEALER

WRITTEN BY
ROANNA BALETA
roannabaleta4@gmail.com

COPYRIGHT (C) 2023

ISBN: 978-978-799-598-3

Published by:

COMMUNE WRITERS INT'L
www.communewriters.com
+234 8139 260 389
6, Amusa Street, Agodo-Egbe, Lagos

Published in the Federal Republic of Nigeria

CONTENTS

Dedication
Acknowledgement
Introduction

Chapter 1: What is Health?

Chapter 2: Can God Really Heal Me?

Chapter 3: You Can't Allow Your Divine Health to Be Snatched Away by Sickness.

Chapter 4: The Fear of Sickness

Chapter 5: Destroying the Fear of Sickness

Chapter 6: Sickness is a Spirit

Chapter 7: I Am the Lord Who Heals

Chapter 8: Don't Limit God and Miss Your Healing

Chapter 9: Healing is a Choice

Chapter 10: Proof That God Can Heal You

About the Author

DEDICATION

This book is dedicated to the sick. God loves you and wants you healed. I can't tell you enough of how much He loves you. It is beyond measure, beyond boundaries and beyond the universe itself. When I felt that love, my heart almost burst.

The love of God is massive.

ACKNOWLEDGMENT

Firstly, a big shout out to God! Then to my awesome dad who never got tired of getting me books and who taught me the ways of the Lord; this is the product, Dad!

To my friends, Goodnews and Co., thank you for your love and support. And special thanks to Pastor Taiwo and Pastor Isaac; I owe you my heart. Thanks a million!

INTRODUCTION

Brethren, bringing you this from the Holy Spirit makes me happy.

You are about to be released from the yoke of sickness by the Lord. This book was written to heal the sick. It is a remarkable manifestation of the healing power of the Holy Spirit. After reading this book, you won't ever get sick again.

The world is sick and abounds in trepidation. When we hear someone die of sickness, we get gripped by fear, saying; "Oh, that person died of this, this person died of that"; we get scared for nothing. For instance, we all know about cancer and how it kills. When we hear someone has cancer, we get terrified instead of declaring our healing over that illness.

This shows we lack knowledge about who we are in Christ and the God we have. Therefore, He is saying; "Sons, I am the Lord, your healer!"

God is the healer and He has revealed to us ways to get healed. He has given us mastery over illness. Matthew 10:5-8; *These twelve Jesus sent forth, and commanded them, saying, Go not into the way of the Gentiles, and into any city of the Samaritans enter ye not: but go rather to the lost sheep of the house of Israel. And as ye go, preach, saying The Kingdom of heaven is at hand. Heal the sick, cleanse the lepers, raise the dead, cast out devils: freely ye have received, freely give.*

As Christians, when someone is sick, we are obliged to know what to do by affirming our healing in Christ Jesus. If a colleague or a neighbour is sick, we should get them healed by proclaiming our authority over sicknesses and diseases, and also by engaging our faith with theirs.

Here is a deep understanding I received from the Holy Spirit: if someone is sick, we can get them healed by bringing them into our reality; our reality of healing, health, and wholeness. Jesus does not only heal, He makes us whole too, just as we saw in the story of the ten lepers. Luke 17:17-19; **And Jesus** *answering said, were there not ten cleansed? but where are the nine? There are not found that returned to give glory to God, save this stranger. And he said unto him, Arise, go thy way: thy faith hath made thee WHOLE.*

By way of illustration, our reality as Christians is that no sickness has authority over us. Hence, when we ask someone to declare and believe that they are healed, we are bringing them into our reality of different dimensions of healing. Mark 4:11; *And He said unto them, Unto you it is given to know the mystery of the kingdom of God; but unto them that are without, all these things are done in parables;*

The blessings of the kingdom are coded; concealed for the benefit of believers. All that appears is not all that exists, so we must commit to knowing those things that are freely given to us, to take full advantage of the diverse provisions in the kingdom, of which our health is not an exception. Accessing good health in the kingdom requires a deliberate commitment to understanding the ways of the kingdom. Psalms 103:7; *He made known His ways unto Moses, His acts unto the children of God.*

The goal of this book is to reveal to us the mystery behind the health of God's people. This mystery has been handed over to us to deal with any form of ailment, irrespective of its name or source. Revelation 1:18; *I am he that liveth, and was dead; and behold, I am alive forevermore, Amen; and have the keys of hell and of death.*

In this book, you will be shown the ways through which God heals.

I am the Lord, that healeth thee,
I am the Lord your healer;
I sent My words to heal your diseases,
I am the Lord your healer.

If you know this song, sing it wholeheartedly.

"Sweet Holy Spirit of God, I bless your name. You are beautiful and mighty, Lord. I asked that you take control and fill the heart of this beloved holding this book. Let your word be activated in his spirit; heal and cleanse anything that is not of God in this body; and most of all, fill his heart with your love, your undying love. Precious Jesus, I ask that you take over. Take over, Lord. You are the healer and the peacemaker. Thank you, Lord Jesus."

Daughter of Zion and son of the mighty God, having this book with you proves that you are set for your healing today.

It shows you are preparing your heart for the great healer to make you whole. You might have tried different methods to get healed. You might have taken lots of treatments and visited different hospitals, and yet nothing is working.

I want you to know that the only person who can heal your body, soul, and spirit is Him. He will give you rest and peace. He is the only healer, and you must recognize Him as such before you can receive your healing. Recognize God as your healer, not the doctor, not the drugs but Him as the Lord that healeth thee.

Firstly, you must know this man before He can unleash His healing ministrations on you. That man is the Holy Spirit—the Spirit of God. It is the Spirit that quickens our mortal bodies and gives us life. See what Roman 8:11 says: *But if the Spirit of him that raised up Jesus from the dead dwell in you, he that raised up Christ from the dead shall also quicken your mortal bodies by his Spirit that dwelleth in you.*

So your life and your health were involved. It is a vital part because God wants us to be healthy. He wants to give us life in our flesh and dominion over sickness and diseases.

He is our Father, and He despises to see us under the oppression of sickness and diseases. He wants us free from every bondage of sickness. He wants you free! He hates seeing you in pain! He wants to give you the power and the key over that sickness that is tormenting you. He said so in Luke 10:19, *"Behold, I give unto you power to tread on serpents and scorpions, and over all the powers of the enemy, and nothing shall by any means hurt you."* God's beloved, He has given you the power. It is up to you to believe the word and receive it for your healing to come forth.

According to His words in Luke 10:19, He said, "I have given you power over the enemy". Sickness is a weapon of the enemy, and the enemy's (Satan's) aim is to kill, steal, and destroy. For everyone who is sick, the enemy has come to steal your health, destroy your healthy body, and then kill it.

It might sound harsh, but the enemy's aim is to kill you. Sickness kills!

The devil doesn't want to steal or destroy your health alone; he wants to kill you. That is the reason he takes it slowly, by giving you little symptoms of illness and allowing them to get worse gradually, from something little to something chronic. He is a smart serpent that kills slowly. The result of that little feverishness is to kill you!

You may think it's a joke, but Satan isn't here for jokes.

Hence, Jesus Christ is saying, "Beloved, I have given you powers over the enemy". Sickness is the enemy's weapon; therefore, Jesus Christ has given you power over the sickness afflicting you. Do you believe that? Many of us find it difficult to believe. Sometimes in our minds, we say, "Is it that easy?" Yes, it is!

It is easy and less stressful. It costs nothing. It is a different dimension that does not require you to spend a dime to get yourself healed. Matthew 11:28-29: *Come unto me, all ye that labour and are heavy laden and I will give you rest. Take my yoke upon you, and learn of me; for I am meek and lowly in heart: and ye shall find rest unto your souls.*

CHAPTER ONE

WHAT IS HEALTH?

Behold, I wish above all things that thou mayest prosper and be in health, even as thy soul prospereth. 3 John 1:2.

In my definition, health is a state of complete physical, mental, and spiritual well-being and the absence of disease or infirmity. Having good health is far better than wealth; being healthy is like having a treasure. There are lots of people in this world that would rather trade their wealth for health because it is so important.

The word "healthy" is one that many of us struggle with. It has seven letters, but it is the most priceless word in existence. Unlike all other things, you can never trade it. Wealth can be exchanged, but your health can never be exchanged — unless you don't love your life.

Those who have perfect health are unaware of the wealth they possess. Many people would give up their fortune simply to be rescued, but I have met people who are wealthy and healthy but are ungrateful.

What use is riches if you keep spending it on illness? Everything would be in vain. So, friends, it is a great thing to be healthy and to be grateful for it.

My uncle was an accountant who worked for a well-known wealthy man while I was growing up in his house. The man was so wealthy that losing three businesses would not make him bankrupt. He had everything, but there was one thing none of his money could buy; good health.

After I finished praying in my room one day, my uncle informed me that he had died. My chest tightened as soon as I heard the news. I had no idea he was ill; I was a student, and all I could think about was my studies.

I inquired as to why he had abruptly passed away. The news was depressing and awful. According to him, cancer was the cause of his death. A well-liked dude! He definitely would wish to swap all his fortune for good health when he was ill, but that was impossible. Wealth can never be used to purchase wellness. Because of this, health is the most prized commodity in the world.

There is so much to be thankful for if you are healthy. You have every reason to honour and glorify God.

God wants us to be healthy. 3 John 1:2; *Beloved, I wish above all things that thou mayest prosper and be in health, even as thy soul prospereth.*

As we succeed in other aspects of our lives, He wants us to be healthy. He wants us to be well so that we can serve Him. Being ill prevents you from serving God as you ought to, and God detests your illness.

Many people are pleading to be released from the shackles of illness. They desire good health. They are aware of its importance. You won't be useful if your body isn't whole. Every day and night, countless people cry out to be healed. I cried all night during one of my nightly prayers when I sensed the Lord's burden for ailing people. I can firmly state that God is not happy that you are sick. He is troubled and He wants you to get well.

I once visited a hospital with a group of friends. I've never been a fan of the smell of hospitals. Everyone dislikes it, I'm sure. It emits the scent of disease that informs you that only the ill are permitted to be there. I had to go since we were in groups.

We were immediately struck by the typical hospital odour when we arrived. We moved on to the additional rooms, and that was when we noticed folks suffering from various devilish ailments, but that was the least of our worries. An accident victim had to have one of his legs amputated because of the damage. He collapsed on the bed in excruciating pain, and from what I can recall, one of his legs was hanging.

Friends, this book will cure you of all your ailments and restore your health. He gave you His word in Isaiah 53:4-5: *Surely he hath borne our griefs, and carried our sorrows: yet we did esteem him stricken, smitten of God and afflicted. But he was wounded for our transgressions, he was bruised for our iniquities: the chastisement of our peace was upon him, and with his stripes, we are healed.*

You will be restored to full health by the great physician, irrespective of the ailment. You will be healed by the power of God's word. It's now time for you to get well and be whole. God has acknowledged that you have endured enough. Jesus sent me to bring His healing words to set you free, and that is why I am here.

The following inquiries ought to be running through your mind right now if you have this book in your hand and are prepared to be healed:

How Can I Be Healthy? What are the Ways?

Friends, God, the Father of our Lord Jesus Christ, is the only way to being healthy. He bestows miraculous health, after all, being ill never makes God happy. He cares for you and does not want to witness your suffering.

See what the Bible says in 2 Corinthians 1:3-4: *Blessed be God, even the Father of our Lord Jesus Christ, the Father of mercies and the God of all COMFORT; who comforteth us in all our TRIBULATION, that we may be able to comfort them which are in any trouble, by the comfort wherewith we ourselves are comforted of God.*

God wants to comfort us during every trial. He wants to be the shoulder you cry on and cling to. But to fall under these provisions, you must confess Him as your Lord and Saviour. You are entitled to all of God's resources for your health if you are saved in Christ Jesus. As His child, He grants you that privilege. John 1:12 says: *But to all who did receive him, who believed in his name, he gave the right to become children of God!*

Friends, to become His child, you must receive and accept Him as your Lord, to be qualified for the benefits He has planned for you. Accepting Him requires that you believe in your heart and confess Him with your mouth. Romans 10:9-10: *Because, if you confess with your mouth that Jesus is Lord and believe in your heart that God raised him from the dead, you will be saved. For with the heart, one believes and is justified, and with the mouth, one confesses and is saved.*

Before we move on, let's say a prayer to receive Jesus as our Lord and Savior: "I bless the name of our heavenly Father. I've decided to stick with you going forward so that I can benefit from your provisions as your ward. I accept you as my Lord and Saviour—Jesus Christ—who gave His life on the cross for me. I declare my faith out loud and in my heart. Amen."

Friends, good news! Right now, He is wholly enmeshed in you.

You can now proudly declare your divine health in Christ as a child of God, and benefit from all of His provisions, not only those related to health. Isaiah 53:5; *But He was wounded for our transgressions, He was bruised for our iniquities; the chastisement of our peace was upon Him, and by His stripes, we are healed.*

Brothers, we were made whole by His stripes. He has already bestowed good health unto us. Now, start cursing every disease in your body. Since Jesus Christ has already paid the price, no disease from the pits of hell is allowed to torture you.

Let me tell you a story of how I experienced a sudden illness. No matter the medications I used, I never felt better. It was rather becoming more serious. I was suddenly struck down with a severe headache I had never experienced in my entire life.

My head was hurting so terribly that I couldn't move because it felt like my brain was about to explode. I thought I was going to pass out from the headache. Mind you, I've heard of headache-related fatalities.

I was taking meds, but I was not getting any better. I kept throwing up everything I ate. Friends, I was in such excruciating pain that I was at a loss for what to do and yearned only to return to normal health. Peace comes from being healthy. I was not at peace with myself.

I was, however, tired of being unwell. The Holy Spirit then began to minister to me. "Rise and pray," He commanded. I heard the voice and complied, but I was unsure of where to begin or how to announce my healing. He then told me to visit YouTube to watch healing-related videos, so I did. I opened the app and looked up Kenneth Copeland, my favourite minister.

I gave one of his messages on healing a quick listen. "Jesus is in this body, and at the mention of His name, every knee shall bow", I shouted as I stood up. So I commanded the illness; "Bow down to Jesus in this body!"

I proclaimed that Jesus dwells in my flesh and that any illness I experienced should submit to the Lord. I cannot have Jesus in me and be sick, for it is not possible to serve two masters. Never! That is what the Bible says in Matthew 6:24: *No one can serve two masters; for either he will hate the one and love the other, or he will be devoted to one and despise the other.*

Friends, immediately I received the light from God's word, I rejected the illness. Since illness is the devil's agent, the devil is the master. Thus, I cannot have Jesus in me and have illness in me as my master. It's never going to happen! Darkness and light cannot coexist; one must make way for the other. I recognized the light and announced my healing. My body is only subject to Jesus, not some bloodsucking devil, and only He can take excellent care of it.

Jesus Christ sacrificed His life so that we would have unrestricted access to all blessings, including our health. To know that He is King, after dying, he came back to life. Matthew 27:51-53; *And, behold, the veil of the temple was rent in twain from the top to the bottom; and the earth did quake and the rocks rent; and the graves were opened; and many bodies of the saints which slept arose, and came out of graves after his resurrection, and went into the holy city, and appeared unto many.*

The cost of your recovery was paid by Jesus. He was beaten, stoned and murdered for your benefit, for your recovery. Do you know that?

You are now entitled to healing because you are a child of God. He died because of you. He received 39 stripes of beating because of you. Our illnesses and ailments were all treated by each stroke He took.

Now go ahead and declare that you are healed from whatever you are suffering from; liver damage, cancer, renal disease, heartache, infirmity; call it out!

Inform the illness of the newfound awareness of your rights. You have the right to never become sick. Your divine health is a right. You are healed, declares God.

For your sake, let the devil know that you are aware of Jesus' death. He suffered harm so that you might be well. 1 Peter 2:24; *Who his own self bare our sins in his own body on the tree, that we, being dead to sins, should live unto righteousness: by whose stripes we were healed.*

Jesus Christ has triumphed over the devil. The devil is aware of this and that is why he is attempting to keep you from knowing it, so you won't be able to escape from the bondage of sickness. He desires to cause harm and then kill you. God, however, is opposing. He says,

"This is something I've made available for my sons and daughters over 2,000 years ago, and they must know it."

You are free from that sickness right now in the name of Jesus Christ, who is greater than all names! By the same name, which is above every other name, you are healed of that illness today. I've been healed through the name of Jesus.

Declare that you are now healed, and tell that sickness to its face, let it know you are free. In Christ Jesus, you are in perfect health.

Divine Health is Your Inheritance

Peter, an apostle of Jesus Christ, to the strangers scattered throughout Pontus, Galatia, Cappadocia, Asia and Bithynia, elect according to the foreknowledge of God the Father, through sanctification of the Spirit, unto obedience and sprinkling of the blood of Jesus Christ: Grace unto you, and peace, be multiplied. Blessed be the God and Father of our Lord Jesus Christ, which according to his abundant mercy hath begotten us again unto a lively hope by the resurrection of Jesus Christ from the dead, to an inheritance incorruptible, and undefiled, and that fadeth not away, reserved in heaven for YOU. 1 Peter 1:1-4

Everyone who is born of God has an inheritance from God. According to the Bible, we are given an unfading, incorruptible inheritance when we are born again. Christ's death was primarily intended to save us and grant us an inheritance. Every man's son and daughter have a claim to their father's assets after his passing. It's the same situation now: as Christ died for us, we have a right to share in His inheritance as God's children.

When we were reborn, God Himself—not His possessions—was what we inherited. As a result, we have access to an infinite number of resources because God (our Father) is the owner of everything.

Although it takes a spiritual form, this legacy affects every aspect of our lives. You should know that life is spiritual. Oh yes! What you see in the physical is a manifestation of what is spiritual. Because of this, when anything happens, individuals will often claim that it first occurred spiritually before manifesting physically.

This is being said to inform you of the reality rather than to frighten you, friends. My Aunt mentioned that a friend of hers died in a vehicular accident, and she went on to explain that it wasn't typical and probably had happened in the hereafter. We are therefore living in a spiritual world, not a bodily one. Many people are unaware that this bodily life is only an illusion.

What defines our general state of well-being in life is our spiritual health. Our spiritual health is what determines how well we perform in every area of life. 3 John 1:2 says; *Beloved, I wish above all things that thou mayest prosper and be in health, even as thy soul prospereth.*

Our inheritance in Christ includes everything related to divine health. But it remains unclaimed, because many people are unaware of this.

Some assets belong to a certain family's heirs but have not been claimed till today. Why has no one claimed it? It's because the kids are unaware of it. They are unaware that the money and assets are their inheritance from their father and that they are the rightful owners. Hence, they are unable to claim it. You can't suddenly decide to claim a property without knowing about it.

This was something that a high school friend of mine told me a few weeks ago. We casually talked about Jesus. He stated, "Divine health and healing are all part of this inheritance we have, but we lack the understanding," in one of the issues we covered. **Cornelius Ankamah** is a footballer, and also a devout follower of God.

So how can we, who are God's children, be ignorant of our inheritance? In the Scriptures, there was this unbeliever who was aware of the inheritance Jesus has provided for us. Yet Jesus dismissed her because she wasn't a believer. *"And, behold, a woman of Canaan came out of the same coasts, and cried unto him, saying, Have mercy on me, O Lord, thou Son of David; my daughter is grievously vexed with a devil. But He answered her a word. And His disciples came and besought him, saying, send her away; for she crieth after us. But he answered and said, I am not sent but unto the lost sheep of the house of Israel."* Matthew 15:22-24

Because she wasn't deserving of the inheritance of God's people, Jesus rejected her. She wasn't born again. But despite the disciples' anger toward her, she persisted because of her faith. Jesus then turned to face her.

"Then came she and worshipped him, saying, Lord, help me. But he answered and said, it is not meet to take the children's bread and to cast it to dogs. And she said, truth, Lord: yet the dogs eat of the crumbs which fall from their master's table. Then Jesus answered and said unto her, O woman, great is thy faith: be it unto thee even as thou wilt. And her daughter was made whole from that very hour." Matthew 15:25-28.

From the parable that Jesus told her, '**the children's bread**' is you! You know that you are born again in Christ Jesus. Jesus was explaining that as a child of God, you have full access to healing and His inheritance more than an unbeliever! **'The crumbs from the table'** were like a fingertip of the inheritance she was begging for.

Jesus was proving that we have more access than **'the fingertip'** as a believer, as a child of God.

I want to share some testimonies from several of my schoolmates with you. There was this Christian friend of mine who endured asthma for a long time. He learned more about God and developed his understanding of his rightful inheritance as a child of God.

He recognized that as a child of God, he could not be asthmatic, and thus he was healed; he grasped that concept immediately. He has been asthma-free up to this point! He used to bring gallons of herbs to school to prevent an asthma attack, but since he realized this truth, he never had an asthma attack again!

Another friend had an eye condition, and just like the first, when he recognized he had control over illness as a son of God, he threw his glasses into the trash, and that was the beginning of his recovery. He never needed it again!

Friends, the wonderful news is that your eyes have been opened as of today. You now understand your heritage in God. You won't get sick ever again. It is part of what you have inherited.

CHAPTER TWO

CAN GOD REALLY HEAL ME?

And said, if thou wilt diligently hearken to the voice of the LORD thy God, and wilt give ear to his commandments, and keep all his statues, I will put none of these diseases upon thee, which I have brought upon the Egyptians: for I am the LORD that healeth thee.
Exodus 15:26.

You know what He said in Exodus: "I am the Lord who heals." So, dear friends, there is no doubt that God can heal you, regardless of your illness. He is a superb doctor!

I used to wonder how God healed people while I was growing up. At that time, I was ten years old, so my religiosity was at a lower level. Oh yes! When I was young, I have known about God. Yet, I began to question how He was able to heal individuals. Then, I started listening to testimonies from members of the church, including the dead ones who came back to life.

I'll share with you some of the testimonies I heard from the minor ones to the major ones. Every testimony is a great honour, and God alone should receive all the praise. I heard a woman's testimony who was told by her doctor that due to the damage in her womb, she would never be able to give birth. Thank God for faith because she returned home and prayed. She knew the God she serves, so she didn't believe the doctor's report.

Dear friends, she heard God's voice while praying for lost souls and preaching the gospel. She was busy doing her Father's business. She took her mind off the doctor's report and decided to obey God's commandment.

Friends, believe me when I say that the same doctor verified her pregnancy the next time she visited the hospital. He also confirmed that she has a brand new womb (our Father has tons of extras!). He would give you a brand new organ for your damaged one. Only the great physician has the power to do that!

Do you understand what just transpired there? Hearing His voice was all it took. "Do my business, and I will settle your business," God stated. See what 1

Thessalonians 4:11-12 says: *And that ye study to be quiet, and to do your own business, and to work with your own hands, as we commanded you; that ye may walk honestly towards them that are without, and that ye may have LACK of nothing.*

Friends, you need to pay attention to God's voice to receive healing.

There was a brother who died but was raised to life by the power of God. He passed away and was transferred to the mortuary, where a lot of chemicals were applied to his body — enough to kill someone who was still alive. His family heard God's voice. Rather than grieving, they entered into streets and began evangelizing, while their brother was in a mortuary.

After completing their missionary work, one of his brothers went to the mortuary to visit the deceased. The brother was told by the diener that there was no hope for him. But he told her, "I serve a living God". The woman grinned and allowed him to view his deceased sibling. They brought the body and placed it on the ground.

He said, "Jesus Christ is right here; get on your feet!" while kneeling next to the corpse. He said this three times, and all of a sudden, the brother who had been poisoned with hazardous chemicals and was dead, woke up. He regained consciousness!

Do you still question God's ability to heal you? Check out the Bible's description of a dying girl and a sick lady. Matthew 9:18-26; *While he spake these things unto them, behold, there came a certain ruler, and worshipped him, saying, my daughter is even now DEAD: but come and lay thy hand upon her, and she shall live. And Jesus arose, and followed him, and so did his disciples. And, behold, a woman, which was diseased with an issue of blood twelve years, came behind him, and touched the hem of his garment: for she said within herself, If I may but touch his garment, I shall be whole. But Jesus turned him about, and when he saw her, he said, Daughter be of good comfort, thy faith hath made thee whole. And the woman was made whole from that hour. And when Jesus came into the ruler's house, and saw the minstrels and the people making a noise, he said unto them, give place: for the maid is not dead, but sleepeth. And they laughed him to scorn. But when the people were put forth, he went in, and took her by the hand, and the maid arose. And the fame hereof went abroad into all that land.*

Yes! God can heal you. He shows no mercy to whatever sickness that is holding you down. And today you are getting healed! God is taking away any sickness destroying your body.

Come on now, let's show you your identity. Do you think, as a child of God, you don't have an identity? You have an identity in Christ. The devil is working hard to hide that fact from you because he knows if you are aware of who and what you are in Christ, you will dominate him and bruise his head.

I found a verse that declares, "I am a co-heir with Jesus." I realized, after reading that verse, that I am like Jesus and what cannot happen to Him cannot happen to me. God spoke about this in Romans 8:16-17; *The Spirit itself beareth witness with our spirit, that we are the children of God: and if children, then HEIRS; heirs of God, and joint-heirs with Christ; if so be that we suffer with him, that we may be also glorified together.*

Therefore, since sickness could not hold Jesus back, it also cannot hold you back. It has no right at all.

Who You Are in Christ

I am crucified with Christ: nevertheless I live; yet not I, but Christ liveth in me: and the life which I now live in the flesh I live by the faith of the Son of God, who loved me, and gave himself for me. Galatians 2:20.

You will not know who you are in Christ if I don't discuss His death and make you understand why He died for you. Before He died for your sins, He settled you with a sickness-free life. When He was beaten countless times, that was you being freed from sickness and diseases. Jesus has completely settled everything for you.

He died to give you proof, evidence, and conviction of who you are. I met a little girl some days ago, and I knew whose child she was. She was the child of the governor of my state, and I went with my dad to visit them. While her dad was discussing with my dad, I decided to make her my friend. So I approached her and asked what her name was, but she glared at me with a look that said, "Who is this asking for my name?"

I waited for her to tell me, and when she finally did, she said, "Do you know who I am? I am the daughter of the governor!", and I smiled. She knew who she was. She was a little girl, but she was aware of the power her dad holds.

Don't you realize who you are, now that your father is the King of all kings? The Most High's daughter or son! Let me tell you something, Satan will take advantage of the fact that you don't know who you are to mess with you.

Many people do not know who they are, even in the physical world. They define themselves by their situations. People define themselves by poverty because they think they are poor. Even in schools, people define themselves by failure, or based on what they hear from others. Let me scream this out loud: that is not who you are!

The devil is trying to deceive you and make you miserable. He wants you to feel less of yourself, put you in a depressed state, and then kill you. He wants to continue to keep you in the dark, but no! Jesus has taken care of that for you. He has given you a real definition of "who you are," and that is who you are, whether the devil likes it or not!

Friends, physically and spiritually, Jesus has given us a new identity. A permanent one! *"But ye are a chosen generation, a royal priesthood, an holy nation, a peculiar people; that ye should shew forth the praises of him who hath called you out of darkness into his marvellous light: which in time past were not a people, but are now the people of God: which had not obtained mercy, but now have obtained mercy."* 1 Peter 2:9.

We were in the bottomless pit until Jesus came to rescue us. He brought us out and took us with Him. He took us to a height that is far above principalities and powers. Ephesians 1:20-21: *Which he wrought in Christ, when he raised him from the dead, and set him at his own right hand in the heavenly places, far above all principality, and power, and might, and dominion, and every name that is named, not only in this world, but also in that which is to come.*

The devil will therefore treat you like trash if you do not know who you are. He'll deal with you and make a mess of you. Let me tell you a story.

One day, I slept during the day as soon as I finished praying. I felt attacked while sleeping. I felt a weight on me. It was like unseen hands were squeezing my neck.

I woke up immediately and became aware that it was an attack from the devil. But because I knew who I was, I got to my feet and began to curse the devil and the forces that pressed me down. I sent them back to the pit of hell, right where they belong. The book of Jude shows that they belong in the pits and I was far above them. Jude 1:6; *And the angels which kept not their first estate, but left their own habitation, he hath reserved in everlasting chains under darkness unto the judgement of the great day.*

This shows that they are ready to oppress you if you lack knowledge of who you are.

We have a new name and a new identity in Christ. See what the bible says in 2 Corinthians 5:17; *"Therefore if any man be in Christ, he is a new creature: old things are passed away; behold, all things are become new."* God is reminding you that He understands you when those voices tell you that no one understands you. God replies, "I'm here for you; you can speak to me" when you feel terrible and no one understands the message you are trying to pass across.

I once stayed with my aunt in another city for nearly five years. When people say "home will always be home," they are saying the truth. Nothing compares to being home. When I was with my aunt, it never felt like home.

I started attending school there, and every time I went, I had a phobia when talking with people and felt the pressure of the classroom. I was terrified of people; I'm not sure why, but it was a major challenge for me.

Another problem would arise when I get home because my aunt was constantly whining and never satisfied with anything I did.

She was a chronic whiner. I made efforts to win her approval, but despite my efforts, she never stopped grumbling. You can imagine the pressure I was under at school and home. Nobody bothered to inquire about my well-being, not even my aunt, who was unconcerned. I didn't have any friends in school but God was with me. He prevented me from feeling down and melancholy.

When the stress became unbearable, I would pray and cry to God. Nobody knew I was struggling because I would cry all night in my room. Nobody was aware that I was under pressure at school as well; it was too much for me. Thankfully, I had God.

Other times, I was too afraid to sleep. I don't remember why, but I was afraid to go to sleep in my room. But then I remembered that I had God. I spoke to Him because I knew He would always be there whenever I needed Him.

I prayed, "I don't know why, Father, but I'm afraid of falling asleep. Would you please stay with me and watch me sleep?" When I prayed, I was in tears. But before I knew it, dear friends, I dozed off. I felt Him assure me that He was beside me. That night, I felt God supporting me, like a mother would to her young baby. I was and still am, God's baby, of course. My life is a practical example of God's love and care.

Now in terms of being oppressed by the devil (through sicknesses and diseases), let him know who you are. Ephesian 2:6-7; *"And hath raised us up together, and made us sit together in heavenly places in Christ Jesus: that in the ages to come he might shew the exceeding riches of his grace in his kindness towards us through Christ Jesus."*

Even an unbeliever took advantage of who Jesus Christ was. There was a centurion in the bible who understood who He was in Matthew 8:5-8: *Now when Jesus had entered Capernaum, a centurion came to Him, pleading with Him, saying, 'Lord, my servant is lying at home paralyzed, dreadfully tormented.' And Jesus said to him, 'I will come and heal him.' The centurion answered and said 'Lord, I am not worthy that you should come under my root. But only speak a word, and my servant will be healed.*

Therefore, knowing who we are, is knowing who Christ is. This man understood that once he gets a word, his servant would be free. This is your true identity in Christ; knowing who you are and living by it!

Jesus has taken us from death to life. 1 John 5:11; *And this is the record, that God hath given to us eternal life, and this life is in his Son.*

Sickness is a gradual, progressive death, and if you don't know this, you will think it's normal and subject yourself to it. If you don't resist it, you will accept it as a norm, because you don't know that is not the way you were supposed to live. James 4:7; *Submit yourselves therefore to God. Resist the devil, and he will flee from you.*

You have left death and entered into life. We don't experience headaches, and even if you feel one, you wouldn't describe it as such. If we feel it, we will rebuke it and order it to leave.

You don't mention you have a stomach ache; you just feel it. You recognize it and rebuke it by saying, "In the name of Jesus, I am normal!"

The Help of the Holy Spirit to Live in Christ

For to be carnally minded is death; but to be spiritually minded is life and peace. Because the carnal mind is enmity against God: for it is not subject to the law of God, neither indeed can be. So then they that are in the flesh cannot please God. But ye are not in the flesh, but in the Spirit, if so be that the Spirit of God dwell in you. Now if any man have not the Spirit of Christ, he is none of his. And if Christ be in you, the body is dead because of sin; but the Spirit is life because of righteousness. Romans 8:6-9.

You need the Holy Spirit to guide you daily and teach you profound truths about God now that you are aware of who you are in Christ. Before leaving the disciples, Jesus assured them that a comforter would arrive as soon as He was gone. The Holy Spirit is that comforter.

The Holy Spirit was given to us by God and sent through Jesus Christ. He was sent to always be with us, and He resides in us. In John 15:26-27; *But when the comforter is come, whom I will send unto you from the Father, even the Spirit of truth, which proceedeth from the Father, he shall testify of me; and ye also shall bear*

The role of the Holy Spirit is to make us more like Christ and elevate Him in our hearts. Without the aid of the Holy Spirit, the life we have in Christ cannot be made manifest as the Lord desires.

We need the help of the Holy Spirit to carry out our roles in Christ after realizing who we are. The Holy Spirit resides within us to serve as a constant reminder of who we are in Christ.

Many of us lack the Holy Spirit's gift of language, which is the gift of prophecy. Even though they believe in the Holy Spirit, some people do not think they can speak in tongues. The gift of speaking in tongues is the product of the Holy Spirit. You can't have one and leave the other, the two are essential.

While in the fellowship, I once had a friend who said that having the gift of tongues is about luck. She was mistaken, I assured her, because everybody who believes in the Holy Spirit is capable of speaking in tongues. And it's in each of us. Activating the gift within you is what you are not doing.

The gift of the Holy Spirit is simple to receive. All you have to do is "fellowship"; complete communion with the Holy Spirit. I'll explain how, at the age of 14, I received the gift of the Holy Spirit.

The things of God have always been my passion. I love to fellowship with Him and sing praises to His name.

I love pouring my heart to Him, crying to Him, and feeling Him. His presence is everything! It feels like a drug, and that is the only drug I want to be addicted to forever (His presence).

I fellowshipped at the Winners headquarters in Ota, Ogun state at that time. Service was awesome and Papa (David Oyedepo) preached. There was a booklet we always receive in the church to pray with. We call it the "Kingdom advancement prayer". I was given mine and decided to pray with it once I got home.

I got home, did all my chores before I went into my room and shut the door. I began to sing praises to His beautiful name. Friends, I was in the mood of worship when I felt something like a downpour. I began to blast in tongues for the next few seconds!

I spoke in tongues for the first time for two hours. I wasn't able to stop myself until my aunt came into the room. I can still remember the way she spoke. She said, "Lord, I know you want to use her. Be calm now, please." Because I was interrupted, I was able to calm down and stop myself. So friends, that was how I got mine, and you can get yours so easily too. You just need to fellowship with an open heart.

Friends, know that the Holy Spirit is in you, you need Him to defeat the devil and his devices (sickness). *For in him we live, and move, and have our being; as certain also of your own poets have said, for we are also his offspring. Forasmuch then as we are offspring of God, we ought not to think that the Godhead is like unto gold, or silver, or stone, graven by art and man's device.* Acts 17:28-29.

Knowing who we are is not enough until we learn to live in the consciousness, and that is with the help of the Holy Spirit. It has to be nailed to the heart. I got to understand something through one of Bishop David O. Oyedepo's sons. He said, "We need to renew our mind constantly with the Word because the devil comes to steal whatever we have learned."

It is true that, despite knowing who we are, we can get disconnected by the world's situations, such as lack of money, relationship problems, barrenness, sickness, etc. That is why we need the Holy Spirit and to be conscious of Him in us.

Those situations will make you forget who you are in Christ. It will make you forget that you are seated with Christ in heavenly places.

Hence, the devil comes to steal the word of God away from you. Luke 8:11-12: *Now the parable is this: The seed is the word of God. Those by the way side are they that hear; then cometh the devil, and taketh away the word out of their hearts, lest they should believe and be saved.*

It has happened to me. Sometimes when I feel some kind of pain, I forget who I am and that I am not meant to feel any pain. The Holy Spirit would then speak to me, reminding me of who I am. Then I will tell that pain to stop, and it will stop because I know who I am.

I would not tolerate any harassment from the devil, so I had to always be in the consciousness of the Holy Spirit because He knows better. And the Bible says, He will be with me always and will bring all things to my remembrance.

The only way to have a constant company with the Holy Spirit is to be conscious of Him, and that happens through the word of God. Keep in mind that without the word of God in you, you will be carnally minded, and being carnally minded is death, but being spiritually minded is life.

Proclaim Your Dominion Over Sickness

And God said, Let us make man in our image, after our likeness: and let them have dominion over the fish of the sea, and over the fowl of the air, and over the cattle, and over all the earth, and over every creeping thing that creepeth upon the earth. So God created man in his own image, in the image of God created he him; male and female created he them. And God blessed them, and God said unto them, Be fruitful, and multiply, and replenish the earth, SUBDUE it: and have DOMINION over the fish of the sea, and over the fowl of the air, and over every living thing that moveth upon the EARTH. Genesis 1:26-28.

Man was designed to rule. In the beginning, everything was given to man, including authority over all creatures and even monsters on Earth. Whatever it was, man had power over it.

The authority of man was reduced after the fall of man, which was brought about by Satan. Man lost his ability to rule and have dominion; he also lost power, and everything on Earth started to have an impact on him. Before, we could control anything, but now, the heat from the sun and rain started to affect man. As a result, we started to whine about our burns from the sun and our cold from the rain.

The beasts of the earth began to have control over man, including fallen angels, sicknesses, diseases, and harsh weather, all of which tormented man because he lost his power. It was as though a king lost the right to his throne, and began to feel the effect of the world outside the throne, getting affected by everything that attacks his kingdom.

All these things were under man's authority until he lost his throne. But our hope, power, and dominion were restored when the Messiah came to give man the throne and power he lost.

He was a Saviour, and the Saviour is Jesus Christ. He is still the Savior today and forever more! He came and burned up everything tormenting man with His unquenchable fire.

See where John was telling people about whom God has sent to the world, who would sit upon the head of the devil and take up power over everything, including man, and restore man's dominion in Matthew 3:11-12.

I indeed baptize you with water unto repentance: but he that cometh after me is mightier than I, whose shoes I am not worthy to bear: he shall baptize you with the Holy Ghost, and with fire: whose fan is in his hand, and he will thoroughly purge his floor, and gather his wheat into the garner; but he will burn up the chaff with unquenchable fire.

During man's fall, when Jesus Christ had not yet come to restore man's position, the devil was roaming and ruling over the earth. He filled the earth with evil and all kinds of it, to oppress and frustrate man because man was God's creature, created by God Himself. This was the reason the devil hates us till today, and he has set out to destroy us to offend God. He destroys everything that pleases God.

He started operating as the earth's monarch, as he still does today (Satan rules the earth, but the power no longer belongs to him since Jesus' arrival). The power is now restored to us by Jesus Christ! Yet, if you are unaware of this, the devil will come and enslave you as a result of your ignorance. My people are destroyed due to ignorance, the Bible says in Hosea 4:6.

The devil knew there was someone who would defeat him when Jesus arrived in Matthew. However, he was aware that Jesus had come to restore man's authority and to establish Himself as the King over all.

That was why, when Jesus began to fast, the devil came to tempt Him so that He would not fulfil His mission. See what Matthew 4:1-3 says:

Then was Jesus led up of the Spirit into the wilderness to be tempted of the devil. And when he had fasted forty days and forty nights, he was afterward an hungred. And when the tempter came to him, he said, if thou be the Son of God, command that these stones be made bread.

Jesus came to teach us about the dominion He has restored. See in the book of Matthew 7:28–29. *And it came to pass, when Jesus had ended these sayings, the people were astonished at his doctrine: for he taught them as one having AUTHORITY, and not as the scribes.*

Most people still do not know that we now have power over the enemy after Jesus restored it. Sickness is an enemy; death is an enemy! That's what Psalm 110:1–3 says. *The LORD said unto my Lord, Sit thou at my right hand, until I make thine enemies thy footstool. The LORD shall send the rod of thy strength out of Zion: Rule thou in the midst of thine enemies. Thy people shall be willing in the day of thy power, In the beauties of holiness from the womb of the morning: thou hast the dew of thy youth.*

So, everything not planted by God is an enemy.

But while men slept, his enemy came and sowed tares among the wheat, and went his way. Matthew 13:25

Sickness is an enemy planted by the devil; do not accept them; they are your enemies. Put up a fight of faith against them, and they will leave because faith can never be defeated in any battle. When I say put up a fight, you have to challenge that sickness. You can't just sit there and let it torment you.

A lady who was diagnosed with the Coronavirus saw the result of the test. She immediately rejected the result. She screamed, "I am not permitted to be sick! I cannot suffer what others suffer as a child of God! No, doctor, that was somebody's report, not mine." She rejected it immediately, and not a single fear was found in her. She was so daring that she could never have it.

The doctor decided to redo the test by taking another sample of her blood. When the result came out, lo and behold, the test came out negative! The doctor was surprised too. Everyone there had Corona, including her, but she rejected hers immediately.

So, friends, you should not take sickness for granted; exercise your dominion over it. You have dominion, so make use of it. Because you are a child of God, you are different from the rest of the people on this earth. You are not normal; you are different! You are in the world but not of the world, so you cannot suffer what the people of the world suffer.

"And now I am no more in the world, but these are in the world, and I come to thee. Holy Father, keep through thine own name those whom thou hast given me, that they may be one, as we are." That is what John 17: 11 says.

I heard a testimony in church about a woman who was delivered from bone marrow cancer by simply rejecting the report. Whose report shall you believe? The doctor's report or God's report? God's report says you are free, you are healed.

Therefore, declare that you can never take the doctor's report! You shall believe the report of the Lord. It is the real report. Isaiah 53:1 says; *Who hath believed our report? And to whom is the arm of the LORD revealed?*

When you believe the report of the Lord, His hands are stretched out to heal you. He is the healer of all diseases. The only report you should believe is the Lord's; the report that Jesus paid the price for your sickness.

Isaiah 53:4-5; *Surely he hath borne our griefs, and carried our sorrows: yet we did esteem him stricken, smitten of God and afflicted. But he was wounded for our transgressions, he was bruised for our iniquities: the chastisement of our peace was upon him; and with his stripes we are healed.*

This is the account from Jesus Christ; while they were beating him, he paid for your freedom from all sicknesses. Every move He made was for your sake. So, whose report are you going to believe? As you read, scream out your response! That represents your proclamation of a life free from sickness.

1 John 5:4-5 says; *For whatsoever is born of God overcometh the world: and this is the victory that overcometh the world, even our faith. Who is he that overcometh the world, but he that believeth that Jesus is the Son of God?*

We have overcome the world, and from this day, you are about to take up the shield of faith and quench all the fiery darts of the devil. *"Above all, taking the shield of faith, wherewith ye shall be able to quench all the fiery darts of the wicked. And take the helmets of salvation, and the sword of the Spirit, which is the word of God."* Ephesian 6:16-17.

I declare in the name of Jesus that you are free! In the name of Jesus, who is above every other name, no sickness will hold you back!

Challenge the sickness. Declare your dominion over it. You are not ordinary. You are a child of God, and a child of God is god on earth. Your father cannot be sick, and therefore you cannot be sick either.

In the same way, the child of a goat is a goat, and the child of a lion is a lion, a child of God is a god. You are god on earth!

Your Health is Restored

For I will restore health unto thee, and I will heal thee of thy wounds, saith the Lord; because they called thee an outcast, saying, This is Zion, whom no man seeketh after. Jeremiah 30:17.

God's will is to restore your health, and the day has come. This is your hour to be free from sickness. Today is the day you will have your supernatural health restored.

By the fire of His word, every terminal disease shall be destroyed! It can't be in your body! It has no right to be in your body!

Our God is a consuming fire! *"For our God is a consuming fire."* Hebrews 12:29.

The great healer is here to heal you now. Expect every shaft and plague of diseases to come to an end.

"God's will is to restore health to me and heal me of my wounds." Say it out loud!

CHAPTER THREE

YOU CAN'T ALLOW YOUR DIVINE HEALTH TO BE SNATCHED AWAY BY SICKNESS

But thou, O man of God, flee these things; and follow after righteousness, godliness, faith, love, patience,

Your healing requires faith. God has sent His word to heal you; it is therefore your choice to activate your faith. You cannot be healed if you don't have faith. No matter the preaching, you will not get your healing if you don't believe. You have to fight the good fight of faith. It is a battle, and until you are set to win, you won't get healed.

There are lots of people afflicted by sickness; they had to put up a fight to be healed by all means. For instance, the woman with the issue of blood. Let me tell you something; no matter the amount you have spent on your sickness, only Jesus can heal you, and it takes faith to get that done. The woman with the issue of blood has tried all means, she spent all she had to find healing but nothing happened until she encountered Jesus. The moment she heard about Jesus healing the sick, her faith came alive.

And a woman having an issue of blood twelve years, which had spent all her living upon physicians, neither could be healed of any, came behind him, and touched the border of his garment: and immediately her issue of blood stanched. And Jesus said, who touched me? When all denied, Peter and they that were with him said, Master, the multitude throng thee and press thee, and sayest thou, who touched me? And Jesus said, somebody hath touched me: for I perceive that virtue is gone out of me. And when the woman saw that she was not hid, she came trembling, and falling down before him, she declared unto him before the people for what cause she had touched him, and how she was healed immediately. And he said unto her, Daughter, be of good comfort: thy faith hath made thee whole; go in peace. Luke 8:43-48.

Jesus' attention wasn't caught because she touched him. No! Jesus was surrounded by a great multitude; thus, it was unlikely that He would be aware of any touch. It was her faith. Her faith was the key. Her faith touched Him, not her, and she was immediately healed.

Every day is God's day to heal us. The day we believe becomes our day. Every day is God's day concerning your healing. Today is your day to get healed!

Faith is not simply working up a feeling or suppressing doubts, but demonstrating a commitment to the One in whose power we put our trust. Hear this; God is moved by your faith, not your fear.

I came across a statement on faith while reading a book. When I started reading, I doubted whether the author knew what he or she was saying until I got to the last line and everything made sense. What if I told you that God, His word, Jesus, and the Holy Spirit have limitations? Would that surprise you?

Would you be more surprised to learn that the blessings of God are being withheld from His people by neither the devil, atheists, nor false religion? The biggest threat to God's capacity to accomplish great things in our lives can come from you and I. Friends, faith is key! Don't allow the lack of faith to prevent you from being healed. Now is your chance to be healed; make that claim by faith.

Even an unbeliever's faith moved God to release His healing. The centurion in the Bible was an unbeliever, but his faith was so mighty that he didn't need Jesus to follow him to his house to get his servant healed. He asked Jesus to just speak the word.

Matthew 8:8-10; *The centurion answered and said, Lord, I am not worthy that thou shouldest come under my roof: but speak the word only, and my servant shall be healed. For I am a man under authority, having soldiers under me: I say to this man, Go and he goeth; and to another, come, and he cometh; and to my servant, Do this, and he doeth it. When Jesus heard it, he marvelled, and said to them that followed, Verily I say unto you, I have not found so great faith, no, not in Israel. The* centurion used his position of authority to express his faith. True faith is about believing.

Some men in the Bible had faith that their friend would get healed. See how mighty their faith was; they had to bring their sick friend to Jesus through the roof.

Mark 2:1-12;

"And again he entered into Capernaum after some days; and it was noised that he was in the house. And straightway many were gathered together, insomuch that there was no room to receive them, no, not so much as about the door: and he preached the word unto them. And they come unto him, bringing one sick of the palsy, which was borne of four. And when they could not come nigh unto him for the press, they uncovered the roof where he was: and when they had broken it up, they let down the bed wherein the sick of the palsy lay. When Jesus saw their faith, he said unto the sick of the palsy, Son, thy sins be forgiven thee. But there were certain of the scribes sitting there, and reasoning in their hearts, why doth this man thus speak blasphemies? Who can forgive sins but God only?

And immediately when Jesus perceived in his spirit that they so reasoned within themselves, he said unto them, why reason ye these things in your hearts? Whether is it easier to say to the sick of the palsy, Thy sins be forgiven thee; or to say, Arise, and take up thy bed, and walk? But that ye may know that the Son of man hath power on the earth to forgive sins, (he saith to the sick of the palsy,) I say unto thee, Arise, and take up thy bed, and go thy way into thine house. And immediately he arose, took up the bed, and went forth before them all; insomuch that they were all amazed, and glorified God, saying, we never saw it on this fashion."

You can see that God is more concerned about our health than our sins. Tell me, what is that thing that will stop you from receiving your healing today? Absolutely nothing. Not even the devil.

We limit God with our faith. He needs your faith to be moved. Even a faith as tiny as a mustard seed can move God. See what Mark 11:22–24 says; *"For verily I say unto you, That whosoever shall say unto this mountain, Be thou removed, and be thou cast into the sea; and shall not doubt in his heart, but shall believe that those things which he saith shall come to pass; he shall have whatsoever he saith. Therefore I say unto you, what things soever ye desire, when ye pray, believe that ye receive them, and ye shall have them."*

As born-again children of God, we get things done by faith. That is what 2 Corinthians 5:7 says; *"For we walk by faith, not by sight."*

You have not found Jesus if He has not demonstrated Himself in your life. See a leper, who was healed because he believed that He could heal him. *"When he was come down from the mountain, great multitudes followed him. And, behold, there came a leper and worshipped him, saying, Lord, if thou wilt, thou canst make me clean. And Jesus put forth his hand, and touched him, saying, I will; be thou clean. And immediately his leprosy was cleansed."* Matthew 8:1-3.

Move God today with your faith, friends. My faith has once brought me healing. Rib aches always stopped me from breathing once they start. Anytime I'm hooked by my rib, breathing becomes quite tough. I returned from church one day and decided to end the misery. I touched it and uttered, "I am healed in Jesus' name! I would not endure this pain anymore!" I declared with faith. Friends, since that day, I have fully recovered from that condition. I no longer experience rib hooks, and my breathing is normal.

So, today, fight the good fight of faith! Your faith is required, and the Lord will grant you a cure. Isaiah 14:27; *"For the LORD of hosts hath purposed, and who shall disannul it? And his hand is stretched out, and who shall turn it back?"* The Lord's stretched hand is set to heal you today.

All that is required to cause God to extend His hands is your faith. No devil can return His hand when He extends it. Your time to be healed has come!

You can't allow the devil to snatch away your right to a sickness-free life because of unbelief in the power of God upon your life. Your health issue was settled before you were born, so any attack against your health is a violation of your right. All you need is faith to tap into your healing.

There was a woman called Martha whose brother had died for days, but when she heard about Jesus, she believed her brother would be saved. What a mighty faith!

That was what happened in John 11:27–44. *"She saith unto him, yea, Lord: I believe that thou art the Christ, the Son of God, which should come into the world. And when she had so said, she went her way, and called Mary her sister secretly, saying, The Master is come, and calleth for thee. As soon as she heard that, she arose quickly, and came unto him. Now Jesus was not yet come into the town, but was in that place where Martha met him. The Jews then which were with her in the house, and comforted her, when they saw Mary, that she rose up hastily and went out, followed her, saying, she goeth unto the grave to weep there.*

Then when Mary was come where Jesus was, and saw him, she fell down at his feet, saying unto him, Lord, if thou hadst been here, my brother had not died. When Jesus therefore saw her weeping, and the Jews also weeping which came with her, he groaned in the spirit and was troubled, and said, Where have ye laid him? They said unto him, Lord, come and see. Jesus wept. Then said the Jews, Behold how he loved him! And some of them said, could not this man, which opened the eyes of the blind, have caused that even this man should not have died?

Jesus therefore again groaning in himself cometh to the grave. It was a cave, and a stone lay upon it. Jesus said, take ye away the stone. Martha, the sister of him that was dead, saith unto him, Lord, by this time he stinketh: for he hath been dead four days. Jesus saith unto her, Said I not unto thee, that, if thou wouldest believe, thou shouldest see the glory of God? Then they took away the stone from the place where the dead was laid. And Jesus lifted up his eyes, and said, Father, I thank thee that thou hast heard me. And I knew that thou hearest me always: but because of the people which stand by I said it, that they may believe that thou hast sent me.

And when he thus had spoken, he cried with a loud voice, Lazarus come forth. And he that was dead came forth, bound hand and foot with graveclothes: and his face was bound about with a napkin. Jesus saith unto them, loose him and let him go."

This was the same faith that the brother, whose sibling had been placed in a mortuary and had preservative (toxic) chemicals injected into his body, had, in the first chapter of this book. Friends, God can do great wonders through your faith.

He doesn't want to see your fear, but your faith. Believe in your Father, and He will show you what He can do with His stretched hands. Faith is the key that gives you access to God's provision for you. James 5:14-15;

Is any sick among you? Let him call for the elders of the church; and let them pray over him, anointing him with oil in the name of the Lord: and the prayer of faith shall save the sick, and the Lord shall raise him up; and if he have committed sins, they shall be forgiven him.

Everything depends on your faith; even other people's faith has the power to heal you. Most Christians are unaware or don't even realize that it's sinful to lack faith, but this is a true statement. *"And whomever has doubts will be damned if they consume food because they are not eating out of faith. All that is not done out of faith is sin."* Romans 14:23.

Everything contrary to faith is a sin. Therefore, allow your faith to soar because God has come to heal every disease planted by the enemy.

If you don't have faith, there is no way to access the healing virtue. That was why Jesus asked, "Who just touched me?" because He felt the healing virtue leaving him. He said out loud, despite the multitude surrounding him, that someone had taken the virtue by faith. It was the woman with the issue of blood. This is faith!

Keep Your Healing

While he yet spake, there cometh one from the ruler of the synagogue's house, saying to him, Thy daughter is dead: trouble not the Master. But when Jesus heard it, he answered him, saying, Fear not: believe only, and she shall be made whole. Luke 8:49-50.

After you have been cured, the enemy (Satan) will return to sow doubts in your heart, but you must keep the demon out with your faith.

The devil employs doubt like a tool to sabotage your testimony. God's healing power cannot emerge in your life once there is doubt in your heart. The devil will try to sow doubts in your heart since he is aware of this and doesn't want you to get healed, but because of your unwavering faith, you can overcome the devil.

See what the Bible says about doubt, *"But let him ask in faith, nothing wavering. For he that wavereth is like a wave of the sea driven with the wind and tossed. For let not that man think that he shall receive any thing of the Lord. A double minded man is unstable in all his ways."* James 1:6-8.

Because the devil doesn't want you to be free, when he sees you are healed, he comes to feed you with doubts. And if you are not firm in your faith, you will become a victim. This is how you stop the devil when he comes to feed you with doubts:

After you get healed, you are excited and filled with joy, and start telling everyone of what the Lord has done. Satan will just sit and watch, thinking, "Oh, she got healed? She thinks she is healed. Well, let's see if she will still think so once I bring back the symptoms," he says as he watches you celebrate your freedom.

He, therefore, shows up with the symptoms at a time you are at peace. You will eventually decide not to celebrate your escape from the illness. Be careful! He created that illusion to see whether you would question the healing you had received.

Why? God says you are healed!

The symptoms return as a result of the devil. When you say; "I can still feel the pain, ouch. I thought I had been healed", you start to have doubts because the devil wants you to. The symptoms stop being an illusion the moment you start to have doubts. The reason these symptoms exist is because you questioned God's ability to heal that sickness.

You don't question your healing; instead, you confront the devil with your faith. For instance, you should declare, "I am healed", and say it to the devil when the pain returns or doubles. Tell him you don't doubt God. There is nothing that can undo what God has said about your healing!

The Bible says, above all, take up the shield of faith. *"Above all, taking the shield of faith, wherewith ye shall be able to quench all the fiery darts of the wicked. And take the helmet of salvation, and the sword of the Spirit, which is the word of God."* Ephesian 6:16-17.

I once said I frequently experienced rib pain, but eventually, I grew tired of having pain all the time. I had to heal myself by using the name of Jesus Christ. Do you know that Satan came to cast doubt in me and make the pain in my ribs twice as bad after I was certain I had been healed?

My response to that was a huge laughter. I laughed because the devil was trying to stop my healing. So I didn't mind the pain at all. The only thing screaming in my head was, "I am healed." I didn't care about the pain because I knew I had been healed. Friends, because of my faith, I was able to get rid of doubt. And today, I am still completely healed from that rib pain!

Papa was telling us about how his wife, Mama Faith David O. Oyedepo, nearly lost her pregnancy due to doubts during one of our church services at Living Faith Church. But because of his faith, the devil couldn't terminate that pregnancy. When he returned home one evening, Mama informed him that she had seen blood, suggesting that the pregnancy had been terminated. Then, he said, "That will never occur! Get my food "and it was over! He rejected it and entirely forgot about the report. And that child was birthed! This is how you dismiss the devil's doubts about your healing.

Thus, friends, you have been healed; do not entertain any doubts from the devil. You must attest to the glory of God!

Instead of having doubts, you should be praising God. Declare that you are healed. If Satan increased the symptoms, scream out; "I am made whole by His stripes! And if I was already healed, then I'm still okay".

The fact that you are healed infuriates the devil, that is why in James 4:7, we are told to keep resisting the devil! *"Submit yourselves therefore to God. Resist the devil, and he will flee from you."*

Divine healing is different from medicine; when God heals you, He doesn't reverse it. You should attest to the power when the symptoms come because the healing power of God remains in you. It will not leave; God never takes back what He gives! He is not like some other gods that ask for things, and when you fail to give, whatever is done is reverted. No! Your God is not like that; freely will He give you and He will never take it back.

It remains because He does it through the power of the gift of healing. If you need healing, you have not lost the power, so testify to that power. When you testify to it, it will come up. How? Look at salvation; it has been given to all men as a gift from God. And God's gift is eternal through Jesus Christ.

If you go back to sin, does it mean that God's salvation has been thrown away? No! The manifestation of life is what you've not allowed to gain supremacy in you. So, awaken it by confession and faith proclamation. Declare, "I am a child of God; I believe in Jesus! And I declare that I belong to Jesus," and when you do that, the word of God is awakened in you.

Sin Can Make You Sick

"For food and water will be scarce. They will be appalled at the sight of each other and will waste away because of their sin." Ezekiel 4:17.

Where illness comes from is a question that many individuals have. Most of the sicknesses are spiritual, whereas only a small percentage are purely physical. There are no two ways to it. The origin of sickness is sin. Adam's sin is the foundation of all sicknesses.

Diseases and other demonic illnesses are born from sin. So, certainly, sin can make you sick as a Christian. The Bible contains several instances of people suffering as a result of their sins.

After this man's sickness was cured, Jesus told him to stop sinning. Once he had been healed, Jesus ran into him again at the temple and warned him about the consequences of sin and told him to sin no more.

"Here a great number of disabled people used to lie, the blind, the lame, the paralyzed. One who was there had been an invalid(infirmity) for thirty-eight years. When Jesus saw him lying there and learned that he had been in this condition for a long time, he asked him, 'Do you want to get well?'

'Sir' the infirmity man replied, 'I have no one to help me into the pool when the water stirred. While I am trying to get in, someone else goes down ahead of me'. Then Jesus said to him, 'Get up! Pick up your mat and walk.' At once the man was cured; he picked up his mat and walked.

The day on which this took place was a Sabbath day, and so the Jewish leaders said to the man who had been healed, 'it is the Sabbath; the law forbids you to carry your mat.' But he replied, 'The man who made me well said to me, 'Pick up your mat and walk.' So they asked him, 'who is this fellow who told you to pick it up and walk?'

The man who was healed had no idea who it was, for Jesus had slipped away into the crowd that was there. Later Jesus found him at the temple and said to him, 'See, you are well again. Stop sinning or something worse may happen to you.' John 5:3-14.

Furthermore, in John chapter 9, Jesus healed a man born blind. The question His disciples asked was, "Who sinned? This man or his parents who claimed that he was born blind." I know it sounds absurd for a child born blind to be asked if he had sinned.

As the disciples thought, the sin should be from his parents; there is no way a newborn child would have sinned. The sin of his parents must be the reason for his affliction. They asked that question because they knew sin could lead to sickness.

If His disciples asked such a question, then it is certain that sin can make us sick. Sin can cause many afflictions, not just sickness. It can make you lose your job; it can make you prone to attacks from the devil; it can make you lose your breakthrough. There are many things it can cause you to lose. And when you sin, the first thing the devil wants to attack is your health.

The devil wants to attack your health so that you will not serve God as you desire, to not fulfil the will of the Father. Hence, sin gives the devil access to ruin your health.

If you had been healed and then went back to sin, that sickness would come back worse. That was why Jesus warned that man in John 5 to stop sinning or something worse would happen to him.

A similar thing happened in Matthew 12, where a person healed of sickness, was warned that it would return and get worse if he resumed his sinful ways.

"When an impure spirit comes out of a person, it goes through arid places seeking rest and does not find it. Then it says, 'I will return to the house I left'. When it arrives, it finds the house unoccupied, swept clean and put in order. Then it goes and takes with it seven other spirits more wicked than itself, and they go in and live there. And the final condition of that person is worse than the first. That is how it will be with this wicked generation." Matthew 12:43-45.

A friend of mine was delivered from the spirit of Satan (a possessing spirit) but went back into sin. The spirit came back worse because she started sleeping with men.

Satan saw it as a privilege to make her miserable. She was sleeping with different men, and hated herself, knowing she could not control the urge. But she called on God, and she was delivered.

Psalm 107:17; *"Some became fools through their rebellious ways and suffered affliction because of their iniquities."*

Flee from sin at all costs because it can be disastrous. Do you think if Joseph had not fled from sin, a greater disaster wouldn't have come upon him? If he had committed that sin, a greater disaster would have come upon him. First from his master, and then from God.

"And after a while his master's wife took notice of Joseph and said, 'come to bed with me!'. But he refused. 'With me in charge,' he told her, 'my master does not concern himself with anything in the house; everything he owns he has entrusted to my care. No one is greater in this house than I am. My master has withheld nothing from me except you, because you are his wife. How then could I do such a wicked thing and sin against God?' Genesis 39:7-9.

He was aware that something bad would happen to him if he sinned against God. He might not have become a prime minister, and he would live a wretched life.

A man won a big contract for his business, but the next day, he lost it because he engaged in fornication. He cried out to God at that point, and God reminded him that his sin had cost him his breakthrough. Psalm 38:3-8;

"Because of your wrath there is no health in my body; there is no soundness in my bones because of my sin. My guilt has overwhelmed me like a burden too heavy to bear. My wounds fester and are loathsome because of my sinful folly. I am bowed down and brought very low; all day long I go about mourning. My back is filled with searing pain; there is no health in my body. I am feeble and utterly crushed; I groan in anguish of heart."

Hence, sin can cause death, both spiritually and physically. And it manifests physically through sickness. The devil wants to kill you, so the first step he takes is to make you sick. And he knows that once you sin, you become prey, and God turns his back on you. Micah 6:13; *"Therefore, I have begun to destroy you, to ruin you because of your sins."*

We fall prey to the devil after we sin. When you become born again, God's protective walls are built around you, but the moment you sin, there will be a crack in those walls. And through that crack, the devil will come in and attack you. The book of Ecclesiastes 10:8 explains it. *"Whoever digs a pit may fall into it; whoever breaks through a wall may be bitten by a snake."* Snake in this context, is the enemy.

I will share my story about sin and its attacks. I used to be a porn addict, and whenever I was done watching it, I would suddenly feel sick from the inside. Physically and spiritually, I would feel down, unlike my usual self. I would feel helpless and miserable. I thought getting some rest would make me feel better and alleviate my guilt. While I dozed off, the enemy began to attack me. I saw forces trying to drag me down; I even tried speaking in tongues, but it was ineffective. My lips were being attacked from speaking in tongues.

But God saved me, and I was able to wake up from that dream. Then the Holy Spirit informed me that I was currently under attack as a result of the sin I had committed earlier. And yes, watching porn is a sin. Do not let anyone deceive you; it is a sin.

It is as though you are willingly submitting yourself to the devil because anything you practice controls you. If you practice sin, it will take control of your life. It implies that you are allowing the devil to rule your life. This is the reason people get addicted to porn; they surrender their control over it, therefore become addicts.

Friends, turn away from sin to be healed and be unaffected by the devil.

Thank the Lord for Jesus, who heals us and pardons our sins. Psalm 103:2-3: *"My soul, praise the Lord and forget not all his benefits. Who forgives all your sins and heals all your diseases."*

To prevent becoming a victim of the devil, avoid sin. As newly born-again people, it is our responsibility as God's children to live a righteous life. God said; be ye holy, for I am holy! Leviticus 11:44; *"I am the LORD your God; consecrate yourselves and be holy, because I am Holy."*

Do Not Run Away from God Because You Have Sinned

We now understand that sin afflicts us and causes God to turn His back on us. Yet, your sin doesn't mean He isn't prepared to accept you as His beloved. First of all, it's wonderful that you are aware you had sinned.

Accepting your sin is a blessing because it opens the door to reconnecting with your heavenly Father, the source. The prodigal son would not have received that loving embrace from his father if he had not realized how far he had gone and how far he had drifted away.

So, sinning is one thing; confessing it is quite another. You are rescued from the pits of sin by this confession. Yes, sin is a pit. And nothing positive emerges from a pit except destruction. But by admitting your sin, you are unlocking the gate of the pit to be let out.

The prodigal son ran back to his father after confessing his wrongdoings. In the same way, when you feel bad about your sin, God is waiting for you to come back to Him. The worst thing you can do is to try to run away from God. The prodigal son would have never returned to his father if he had not made up his mind he would never do so out of shame. God never want you to run away from Him because of your sin. Yes, He hates sin, but He will never cast you away because of it. The way the father cleaned up his prodigal son is the way God is ready to clean you up and make you white as the snow.

Let's look at the parable of the prodigal son. If you feel awful about committing a sin, this is for you. Put yourself in the shoes of the prodigal son and come back to Jesus.

Luke 15:11-17; *And he said, A certain man had two sons: and the younger of them said to his father, Father, give me the portion of goods that falleth to me and he divided unto them his living. And not many days after the younger son gathered all together, and took his journey into a far country, and there wasted his substance with riotous living.*

And when he had spent all, there arose a mighty famine in that land; and he began to be in want. And he went and joined himself to a citizen of that country; and he sent him into his fields to feed swine. And he would fain have filled his belly with the husks that the swine did eat: and no man gave unto him. And when he came to himself, he said, How many hired servants of my father's have bread enough and to spare, and I perish with hunger!

He decided to return to his father at this point, despite the shame! Let's go further to verses 18-20. *I will arise and go to my father, and will say unto him, Father, I have sinned against heaven, and before thee. And am no more worthy to be called thy son: make me as one of thy hired servants. And he arose, and came to his father. But when he was yet a great way off, his father saw him, and had compassion, and ran, and fell on his neck, and kissed him.*

Whoever you are, this is for you. God is ready to hug and kiss you when you run back to him. In verse 21-24; *And the son said unto him, Father, I have sinned against heaven, and in thy sight, and am no more worthy to be called thy son. But the father said to his servants, Bring forth the best robe, and put it on him; and put a ring on his hand, and shoes his feet.*

And bring hither the fatted calf, and kill it; and let us eat, and be merry: for this my son was dead, and is alive again; he was lost, and is found. And they began to merry.

When you come back to your heavenly father, He rejoices this way. He is happy and gladdened by your return. You shouldn't try to run away from God because of your sin; rather, you should cry out to Him and become closer to Him, so that He can help you become clean. Other than Him, no one can make you clean. Only God can redeem you from your sin.

He said; come unto me, and I will clean you up. Isaiah 1:18; *Come now, and let us reason together, saith the LORD: though your sins be as scarlet, they shall be as white as snow; though they be red like crimson, they shall be as wool.*

No matter your sin, He is ready to accept you and make you as white as the snow. Now, despite your sins, God will never allow sickness to torment you. This is why He says, 'I am the Lord, your healer."

God will heal you despite your sin. He will forgive and heal you. Psalms 103:3-4; *Who forgiveth all thine iniquities (sins); who healeth all thy diseases; who redeemeth thy life from destruction; who crowneth thee with loving kindness and tender mercies.*

Thus, dear friends, come back to the Father by telling Him about your sin, and He will pardon and heal you. 2

Chronicles 7:14; *If my people, which are called by my name, shall humble themselves, and pray, and seek my face, and turn from their wicked ways; then will I hear from heaven, and will forgive their sin, and will heal their land.*

I always enjoy sharing my experiences with you. Keep in mind that nobody can offer anything other than what they have personally experienced.

One day, I sinned and became overwhelmed with guilt. I felt like shit, then I cried to my close spiritual friend and told him, "Goody, I did something bad, and I'm overwhelmed with guilt. I won't tell you though, but please, if the Holy Spirit tells you about it, keep it to yourself". I told him this when I was submerged in a sea of guilt.

He laughed because we are so close that the Holy Spirit reveals our personal lives to each other. If something is wrong with me or if I've gone astray a bit, the Holy Spirit tells him. Also, if Goodnews is confused about certain things or does something wrong, the Holy Spirit will tell me too. I don't understand that kind of connection, but that's how it is.

He tried to let me know God still loves me despite my wrongdoings and that I should go to Him. Then I said, "I'm guilty of the fact that I did it again, after promising

God that I wouldn't. I feel like killing myself, Goody. I don't deserve His mercy at all." I cried.

Then I went on to say, "I was thinking my punishment would be that He wouldn't wake me up this morning. But I'm still alive. Goody! I don't deserve this mercy!"

His eyes were a little teary, and he said, "Jesus will help you, Roanna", and I continued with my waterworks. "I can't continue to apologize every time something goes wrong. I hate that He still loves me regardless and shows me mercy. Do I deserve this mercy, Goody?"

He whispered, "Roanna." I tried to pay attention to the tone of his voice. "Jesus is hearing your cry; come back to Him. Don't be afraid."

I was still so drowned in guilt. I didn't know how to apologize again, and he said, "Jesus will always love you, no matter what. Come to him." I heeded those words, and let them play in my head instead of allowing guilt to fill my head. I shut my eyes and cried out to Jesus, asking for forgiveness, knowing that He loved me and was ready to forgive me anytime.

I suddenly felt free from the bondage of guilt. Well, I think I have a good friend for life, always available to bounce me up in my spiritual life. That friend is Goodnews; everyone needs that friend, and I've got mine. Glory be to God.

The Bondage of Sin

Now the Lord is that Spirit: and where the Spirit of the Lord is, there is liberty. 2 Corinthians 3:17.

Someone once asked me why we repeat the same sin. I had no response until I asked the Holy Spirit. Whatever has no freedom becomes a bond. Where the Spirit of the Lord is, there is freedom.

Since sin can never come close to God, there's always freedom in His presence. Sin will never bring you freedom. Anything that has no freedom is a sin. Have you ever seen a thief steal with peace of mind?

Have you ever seen someone lie and not feel guilty about it? This is to show that there is no freedom in sinning. Hence, sin puts you in bondage; a heavy heart of guilt. I have never sinned and not felt guilty about it. If I don't, then it means I'm dead; dead in the spirit.

You are a slave to sin, which is why you keep returning to it. It shows that your carnal mind is in control of your life. The Bible says the flesh and the spirit are always at war. Galatians 5:17; *For the flesh lusteth against the Spirit, and the Spirit against the flesh: and these are contrary the one to the other: so that ye cannot do the things that ye would.*

Is it possible to be free from this bondage? Yes, it is. Through the help of the Holy Spirit, you can be free from the bondage of sin and never repeat it. If you read further in verses 18–25, you will see that the Holy Spirit frees you from the bondage of sin.

But if ye be led of the Spirit, ye are not under the law. Now the works of the flesh are manifest, which are these; Adultery, fornication, uncleanness, lasciviousness, idolatry, witchcraft, hatred, variance, emulations, wrath, strife, seditions, heresies, envyings, murders, drunkenness, revellings, and such like: of the which I tell you before, as I have also told you in time past, that they which do such things shall not inherit the kingdom of God.

But the fruit of the Spirit is love, joy, peace, longsuffering, gentleness, goodness, faith, meekness, temperance: against such there is no law. And they that are Christ's have crucified the flesh with the affections and lusts. If we live in the Spirit, let us also walk in the Spirit. Let us not be desirous of vain glory, provoking one another, envying one another.

I once battled with porn until I caught the light through the Holy Spirit, which enabled me to break free from the bondage. I was blindly enslaved and found it difficult to overcome my addiction.

If you are struggling to be free from the clutches of sin, the Holy Spirit is at your rescue.

He can help you the same way He helped King David in the Bible. King David was a sinner, but when he realized he had sinned against God, he ran back to Him and cried his eyes out, asking the Holy Spirit to help him, which He did, because David never went back to sin. This is the empowerment of the Holy Spirit.

David committed adultery with Bathsheba, then he cried out to God. Let's see Psalms 51:1-11; *Have mercy upon me, O God, according to thy lovingkindness: according unto the multitude of thy tender mercies blot out my transgressions. Wash me thoroughly from mine iniquity, and cleanse me from my sin. For I acknowledge my transgressions: and my sin is ever before me.*

Against thee, thee only, have I sinned, and done this evil in thy sight: that thou mightest be justified when thou speakest, and be clear when thou judgest. Behold, I was shapen in iniquity; and in sin did my mother conceive me. Behold, thou desirest truth in the inward parts: and in the hidden part thou shalt make me to know wisdom. Purge me with hyssop, and I shall be clean: wash me, and I shall be whiter than snow.

Make me to hear joy and gladness; that the bones which thou hast broken may rejoice. Hide thy face from my sins, and blot out all my iniquities. Create in me a clean heart, O God; and renew a right spirit within me. Cast me not away from thy presence; and take not thy holy spirit from me.

Read the entire chapter when you have some free time.

The Holy Spirit helps you do things that are of the spirit and not things that are of the flesh. The Holy Spirit empowered David to not repeat that same sin. David committed adultery in the Bible only once, and he never repeated that act after he cried out to God. This was done through the power of the Spirit of God.

CHAPTER FOUR

THE FEAR OF SICKNESS

"For the thing which I greatly feared is come upon me, and that which I was afraid of is come unto me. I was not in safety, neither had I rest, neither was I quiet; yet trouble came." Job 3:25-26.

Job in the Bible was terrified that a terrible calamity was going to strike him. He was terrified and his worst fears came true.

Another tool the devil employs to imprison and enslave us is fear. He uses it as a tool to undermine your faith. It is that silent voice that has come to steal, kill, and destroy. It is the devil's greatest trick.

When the devil instils fear in your heart, he knows that his work is done. Fear makes you vulnerable to attack. But Jesus is about to change that now!

The devil uses the fear of illness as a tool to enslave people. Why are people afraid of getting sick? It is that power that enslaves you and treats you like prey. That power is what causes you to tremble whenever you hear about someone's sickness, and you'd begin to worry, "What if this happens to me? What if it was a close friend?" That is the voice of fear; that eerie voice, which is silent. It infiltrates your thought, thus you are expected to rebuke it.

Also, if you experience pain in your internal organs, fear begins to crawl into your heart. A friend once confided in me that she was experiencing stomach ache and it was spreading to her chest. She said, "I've been having this weird agony in my heart, and I'm afraid". Her words and face made it clear that she was genuinely afraid.

God knows I disregard such claims, but as soon as I noticed Bella was afraid, I reassured her that she shouldn't be concerned. Do you not recognize who you are? "We would do a check-up to show you that there is nothing wrong with you. Don't fret; everything is OK. You have the name of Jesus, there is nothing to be scared of." She seemed at ease after a while.

When that fear appears and you embrace it, it takes control of every aspect of your life. It won't end there; it will continue to torment you until it manifests itself in your life. Jesus, however, is here to assure you that He did not give you the spirit of fear but the spirit of peace and sound mind. *"For God hath not given us the spirit of fear; but of power and of love, and of a sound mind."* 2 Timothy 1:7.

Fear is a prisoner of destiny. Fear keeps you in the dark and prevents you from seeing the good life that God has planned for you. Meanwhile, fear is just an illusion. It only becomes real when you choose not to correct it.

I watched a Christian movie where a lovely girl was being tormented by the devil and had to lock herself behind the door for days. Every time she tries to open it, a spirit would appear to torture her and tell her lies. She received sermons from several people who, of course, were sent by God. They described to her how lovely the outside world was and how she would keep suffering the torment of fear if she doesn't stand her ground and get out of the dark, nasty room.

Whenever she seems a little convinced, the spirit would creep in again to tell her the lies. Many of you don't know that fear is a spirit. Oh yes! It is a spirit; it is one of the spirits that resides in the bottomless pit of hell.

To continue keeping her in the dark, the ghost approached and convinced her of his numerous lies. She would then become more afraid and reject what her friends had told her. This is the result of her continual acceptance of fear. She was told by the evil spirit that she was nothing and would never be useful, that she was good for nothing and nothing will ever work out fine for her, and she believed it.

If you don't rebuke the devil, he will keep tormenting you with fear. I decided to learn how to swim one afternoon because I like to spend time alone near water. I adore the serenity and tranquillity it brings. So, on the first day of my training, I attempted to swim around on the fourth foot as a starter.

I went the following day, but my coach was late, so I decided to swim on my own because I had done it the first day. When I went into the water, it felt different, as though it was overflowing, but it wasn't. So, before I started swimming, I decided to be balanced in the water. But that eerie, silent voice of fear came as I was getting ready to swim.

"People who could swim have died in a pool before, so don't go in", it said.

"Devil you lie! I cannot die! It is written in Psalm 118:17, "I shall not die but live, and declare the works of the Lord!"

Sometimes you need to quote the scripture to the devil so that he will know that you know it and that you are of God. Immediately I rebuked that eerie voice of Satan, I dived right into the pool and began my swimming session. Satan is a liar, and he will continue to be a big-time liar.

The devil plans to dominate your life with fear so that he can keep God from doing what He wants to do with you. When you are terrified, it will be easy for the devil to attack you. Your health is the first thing the devil targets. Why? Because you were made to use your body to exalt God since it is the temple where God dwells. *"Know ye not that ye are the temple of God, and that the Spirit of God dwelleth in you?"* 1 Corinthians 3:16.

The devil enjoys destroying God's creation. Satan knows that God is exalted in your body, therefore his ultimate goal is to destroy the temple of God by making you sick. And he starts by instilling fear in you.

One of the weapons used to attack believers and nonbelievers is the fear of sickness. The devil has come to sow an evil seed, and if that seed is allowed to develop, it will manifest in that person's life. Fear is one of the most powerful tools Satan can use to harm God's children, and God is aware of this. This is why in almost every book in the Bible, you will see "fear not". It appears about 365 times in the Bible. God states, "Fear not."

This means He is telling us to fear not every day.

He has given you the authority to resist the devil and it shall flee. *"Submit yourselves therefore to God. Resist the devil, and he will flee from you."* James 4:7.

The devil is a master mind manipulator; he is aware that you have triumphed over him in Christ, but he still intends to prevent the situation to deceive you. He is an excellent con artist. He tried to trick Jesus on the mountain in the same way, but Jesus rebuked him. *"Then the devil taketh him up into the holy city, and setteth him on a pinnacle of the temple, and saith unto him, if thou be the Son of God, cast thyself down: for it is written. He shall give his angels charge concerning thee: and in their hands they shall bear thee up, lest at any time thou dash thy foot against a stone. Jesus said unto him, It is written again, Thou shalt not tempt the Lord thy God."* Matthew 4:5-7.

The devil was aware that Jesus Christ had triumphed against him, so he tempted Jesus to turn the situation around. He said since Jesus is the son of God, God would send down angels to catch him if He descend the mountains. How is it possible for a man in charge to listen to a mere slave? The devil is a slave to Jesus.

Hence, friends, you must resist the devil's plans. Sickness cannot be feared. Remember, whenever you are afraid, you are giving the devil permission to rule over you. The devil wants to use fear to make you sick.

This is what the Bible says about fear in Psalm 91:5-16;

"Thou shalt not be afraid for the terror by night; nor for the arrow that flieth by day; Nor for the pestilence that walketh in darkness; Nor for the destruction that wasteth at noonday. A thousand shall fall at thy side, and ten thousand at thy right hand; But it shall not come nigh thee.

Only with thine eyes shalt thou behold and see the reward of the wicked. Because thou hast made the Lord, which is my refuge, even the most High, thy habitation; There shall no evil befall thee, Neither shall any plague come nigh thy dwelling.

For He shall give his angels charge over thee, to keep thee in all thy ways. They shall bear thee up in their hands, lest thou dash thy foot against a stone. Thou shalt tread upon the lion and adder: the young lion and the dragon shalt thou trample under feet. Because he hath set his love upon me, therefore will I deliver him: I will set him on high, because he hath known my name. He shall call upon me, and I will answer him: I will be with him in trouble; I will deliver him, and honour him. With long life will I satisfy him, and shew him my salvation."

Do you still let fear have control over your life despite what the Lord has said? Do you allow the fear of sickness to steal your right to a sickness-free life in Christ? You will never be the same again. The spirit of fear is set to leave you right now in the name of Jesus!

According to Mama Faith Oyedepo, fear is an illusion. Fear is fake evidence appearing real. It is phoney; it is not real. Now rebuke that fear in your heart!

To show you that fear is an illusion, I'll tell you about a scenario. A man was going from his hometown to an unfamiliar location. He was travelling through a forest when he noticed a lion standing in the middle of the road. Overcame with fear, he stopped moving. A lion was blocking all access to the road, and since he had already travelled far, turning around would prompt the lion to pursue and devour him. As a result, he started to sweat profusely and breathe heavily.

He nearly peed on himself as he stood there lifeless. It was going to run after the man and devour him since it was a lion. Also, the lion will gobble him up if he approaches. He decided to embrace his inevitable fate. He started approaching the lion, but the lion remained still. He began to be a little sceptical about the circumstance but he persisted. The lion did not move when he drew near. He felt brave, so he approached closely and touched it; to his surprise, he discovered that it was a statue!

This is to let you know that none of your fears are valid. It is just like the lion statue, appearing as a real lion.

Fear of sickness is dangerous; it is a killer of hope. I read in Dr David Jeremiah's book that when he was diagnosed with cancer, the fear he felt was something he never thought he would recover from. The fear never left when he began his treatment; each time he gets close to the hospital for his check-up, the fear creeps in again. It would make his stomach sick. There was this feeling of grief and fear.

If you are sick, you don't need fear; you need faith to get healed.

I have heard of how people died from the fear of sickness — not that the sickness killed them, but the fear. The year the Ebola virus came, people spread fake news that the best protection against contracting the virus was drinking or bathing in salty water. You know how false news spreads like wildfire. Everyone scared of contracting the virus, began to drink salty water. Some drank it excessively and it began to damage their health. Most people died from the excess salt added to their water.

That is the fear of sickness. They were scared of having the virus, and it made them lose their lives. Didn't your Father in heaven ask you not to fear? As a Christian, how can you be afraid of sickness?

Why will you let the devil sow fear into your life? Haven't you heard that you are in the world but not of the world? So what affects others cannot affect you.

Rebuke every fear you have right now! Don't you know your position? You are seated with Christ in the heavenly places. Now tell me, can a common virus infect someone who is seated with Christ? How dare the sickness! Put up a wall of faith and rebuke that fear. You are above it!

Also, when COVID-19 came, I couldn't believe Christians were scared of contracting it. Of course, it was rampant and extremely contagious, but that doesn't permit you to be infected. I knew people who were so terrified due to the symptoms. The symptoms were similar to malaria or fever, so anyone catching a cold would start having the fear of being infected.

Someone's temperature was a little high, and he started panicking. No! You are not meant to be scared. Don't you know that He who is in you is greater than he who is in the world? He is greater than every virus and sickness.

1 John 4:4, *"Ye are of God, little children, and have overcome them: because greater is he that is in you, than he that is in the world."*

Sickness is part of the world, but you are not of the world. Thus, how can it affect you? An African proverb says, "Who gave snake wings to fly?" Does a snake have wings? No. But why? Because it is impossible. Hence, if it is impossible for a snake to fly, then it is impossible for you to fall sick.

Why will sickness find you? Are you part of the world that sickness belongs to? No! You are not of the world!

The Bible says 'they' not 'you', or 'me' but 'they' are of the world; therefore, they speak of the world. That is, whatever happens in the world only affects the people of the world. It cannot affect us because we are of God. That is what 1 John 4:5-6 says; *"They are of the world: therefore speak they of the world, and the world heareth them. We are of God: he that knoweth God heareth us; he that is not of God heareth not us. Hereby know we the spirit of truth, and the spirit of error."*

How did you read that? According to the Bible, as God's children, we should be able to distinguish between what comes from God and what comes from the devil (the spirit of sickness and fear). Such fear is irrelevant to you; the only fear you need is the fear of the Lord.

I was searching the internet a few days ago for news about COVID-19. I stumbled across a website that discusses news regarding health, one of which is COVID-19. I saw several deaths linked to the vaccine on the website.

As a result of the fear of contracting the virus, you took the vaccine. This is the fear of sickness we are talking about. Also, you weren't a victim of the virus; you just needed to prevent it out of fear, and unfortunately, it brought death. Can you see how fear can mislead and kill you?

Many died out of fear of sickness. You don't need to be afraid when you have a God who can heal you and a God who has assured you to fear not; a God who has defeated sickness for your sake.

The fear of sickness kills faster than the sickness itself. Who gave you the spirit of fear when your Father has not given you the spirit of fear? Why do you fear when you are seated with Christ in the heavenly places? Therefore, in the name of Jesus, I cast out every spirit of fear!

Deuteronomy 1:19-24;

"And when we departed from Horeb, we went through all that great and terrible wilderness, which ye saw by the way of the mountain of the Amorites, as the LORD

our God commanded us; and we came to Kadeshbarnea. And I said unto you, Ye are come unto the mountain of the Amorites, which the Lord our God doth given unto us.

Behold, the LORD thy God hath set the land before thee: go up and possess it, as the LORD God of thy fathers hath said unto thee; fear not, neither be discouraged. And ye came near unto me every one of you, and said, we will send men before us, and they shall search us out the land, and bring us word again by what way we must go up, and into what cities we shall come. And the saying pleased me well: and I took twelve men of you, one of a tribe. And they turned and went up into the mountain, and came unto the valley of Eshcol, and searched it out."

You have to confront fear and understand what causes you to be afraid. Question what you are scared of. You can't run from fear; wherever you show up, fear will be waiting for you at the door. So, friends, you have to confront it!

You have a greater spirit in you that can conquer fear. You do not have to fear; fear nothing. Isaiah 41:10; *"Fear thou not; for I am thee: be not dismayed; for I am thy God; I will strengthen thee; yea, I will help thee; yea, I will uphold thee with the right hand of my righteousness."*

Therefore, do not be afraid of sickness but be joyful always in the Lord. Always give thanks to God, our Father. *"A joyful heart is good medicine, but a crushed spirit dries up the bones."*

You are a child of God; nothing should make you afraid; instead, things should be afraid of you because you are God's own. You are of God and not of the things (same category) of this world. In one of the Sunday services I attended, Papa David O. Oyedepo told the story of how occultists, witches, and powers fear him — even sickness.

He asked one of them a question; why is it that when ordinary people cross the highway, they have accidents and die, but when he does, nothing of the sort happens? The wizard said they can never dream of tempering with him because he (David Oyedepo) has a higher power. The wizard also said, when they want to suck blood at the highway and they sense a higher power coming, they clear off.

Hence, you belong to a higher power because you have your God backing you. See what Joshua 1:9 *"Have I not commanded you? Be strong and courageous. Do not be frightened, and do not be dismayed, for the Lord your God is with you wherever you go."*

I will share where sickness got scared of him (David O. Oyedepo) because he is not of this world but of God.

Sickness should not make you afraid; instead, it should be afraid of who you are, what you carry, and the God backing you.

He heard that one of his cousins had a mental problem. He told them to be calm and would be there soon. Immediately he stepped into the house, he greeted his cousin and he was normal! This was someone who has been misbehaving before he showed up. But as soon as he did, he became normal and his healing was permanent. If you know who you are and what you carry, nothing can scare you. Nothing can torment your body; no sickness from the pit of hell can.

Sickness Can Stir Up Fear

"Behold, I will bring it health and cure, and I will cure them, and will reveal unto them the abundance of peace and truth." Jeremiah 33:6.

Getting scared is losing faith. It has never been easy for those who are sick. Their lives are bound by fear: fear of pain, never being well again, being lame, being blind, being unable to live a normal life with their loved ones, and of death. Getting scared during sickness is the greatest mistake. You do not need fear; you need hope and faith in God.

There is anguish in my heart whenever I hear or see sick individuals. Tears will begin to fall down my cheek when the ache of witnessing people in pain becomes too great. There is nothing I can do to stop the excruciating pains, which I can never bear. I detest the emotion it causes. I am powerless to help them; only God, through the greatness of His love and mercy, can heal them. He is the only one that can set them free from that pain.

I read a story about a guy who was sick. He had suffered for long, from one surgery to another, and was in the hospital for months. This guy survived on the oxygen tank and medications. He spoke for a while, but as the situation got worse, he could no longer do it; he could no longer mouth the words. It was terrible.

The pain in his eyes was obvious, and as the days went by, fear slowly crept into his heart. His eyes were stirred with unease. When asked about his thoughts, his eyes became teary as he said, "I don't understand what God is doing." He gulped roughly, then added, "I'm scared."

This guy's pain is common with sick people. Fear preys on the mind and hearts of those who walk through the doors of a hospital. There's fear lurking around the hands-in-waiting for a surgery or biopsy result. Whatever the circumstances, illness can stir up fears you didn't know you have.

Although medication can dull your pain and therapies can slow down cancer, nothing can heal you or take away such fears. Only God can. Not the drugs, not the therapies, not the surgery! I have seen others go through similar situations yet they still had hope in God, and God saw their faith and healed them out of love. God can do the same for you!

God remains supreme over all the drugs, pathology reports, bad prognoses, and statistics. His love and faithfulness are everlasting; they're never changing. God never take back His word! He is not a doctor and doesn't change his healing theories. He is still the same God.

The books of Malachi 3:6 and Hebrews 13:8 declare that God is always the same and never changes. He will always be good, always be loving, and always be all-powerful. No matter how things change around us, we can trust God to be consistent. He is the same yesterday, today, and forever!

He is independent of the conditions listed in your medical charts. Christ is the perfecter of our faith. That is what Hebrews 12:2 says; *Looking unto Jesus the author and finisher of our faith; who for the joy that was set before him endured the cross, despising the shame, and is set down at the right hand of the throne of God.*

Dr King said in one of Kathryn Kuhlman's books, "I have the highest regard for the medical profession, and from my conversations with doctors, I believe that one cannot be a doctor of medicine and not be religious. It should not be amazing that we have doctors who tell of their personal experiences with their patients. All healing comes from God; a surgeon can perform surgery, but he must wait for a higher power to do the healing; a doctor can prescribe medicine, but it takes God to heal."

Jesus gave His life to save us from the darkest of fears. How can we cling to this truth when fear cages us in the bonds of sickness? This is what you need to destroy fear.

First, we need to give our fears to God. Fear during sickness should prompt us to turn to God in prayer. The Bible doesn't promise us freedom from tribulations but promises that the Lord will hear when we pray to Him. The Bible says in Luke 11:11-13;

"If a son shall ask bread of any of you that is a father, will he give him a stone? Or if he ask a fish, will he for a fish give him a serpent? Or if he shall ask an egg, will he offer him a scorpion? If ye then, being evil, know how to give good gifts unto your children: how much more shall your heavenly Father give the Holy Spirit to them that ask him?"

David in the Bible always run to God each time fear crept into his heart. *"I sought the LORD, and he heard me and delivered me from all my fears."* Psalm 34:4. Paul in the Bible also guides us to pray during tribulations, to pray without ceasing. *"Rejoice evermore. Pray without ceasing. In everything give thanks; this is the will of God in Christ Jesus concerning you."* And Peter encourages us to cast our fears on God because He cares for us. 1 Peter 5: 6-8;

"Humble yourselves therefore under the mighty hand of God, that he may exalt you in due time: Casting all your care upon him; for he careth for you. Be sober, be vigilant; because your adversary the devil, as a roaring lion, walketh about seeking whom he may devour."

I once read about a young girl who prayed for her father suffering from a spinal injury. He had lost one of his thumbs as well. The young girl would pray and sob as she witnessed her father struggling to walk. She would then rush to God and pray, saying, "I have faith that God can heal my dad. Please heal Daddy's pain so he can start walking again and let his thumb come back to life. God, I know you can help Daddy with this. Thank you, Holy Spirit." She prayed constantly, and one day when Daddy had returned from church, the spinal injury had been completely healed, and his thumb came back to life This is the power of prayer through faith. God can heal through prayer.

A doctor made it a routine to pray before every operation. He said he is just an instrument through which God heals, so he prays first before he performs any operation. To my greatest surprise, it works every single time! He understood that people are both materialistic (flesh) and spiritual (spirit) and that God, the great healer, often overrules His natural laws with the supernatural laws of love and mercy and heals miraculously.

Fear blocks healing; refuse fear.

When we prayerfully turn our fears over to God, He takes control of everything with the peace of Christ. As Paul reminds us in his letter to the Philippians; *"Be careful for nothing; but in everything by prayer and supplication with thanksgiving let your requests be made known unto God. And the peace of God, which passeth all understanding, shall keep your hearts and minds through Christ Jesus."* Philippians 4:6-7.

When fears come during sickness, remember you have a God who heals. You cannot have the same sickness as Christ. "I cast out every spirit of fear! And in the name of Jesus, you are healed today!"

A man recalled how praying to God for healing helped save him from death. "I had previously been in danger of dying. I was transported by ambulance to Pembroke

Hospital in severe condition in 1945 due to pneumonia. I recalled the physicians whispering to my wife that I was close to passing away. I prayed fervently. Although I had no fear of passing away, I prayed that I would live long enough to watch my children become adults. The next day, my fever had subsided, and I was able to go home with no side effects. I was healed from pneumonia by the power of God. Thank you, Lord Jesus."

Lastly, our Father gives us the kingdom and therefore eradicates our fears through the redeeming blood of the Son. He embraces us as His children, bringing us under His protective shield when fears creep into us and try to steal our rights as co-heirs of Jesus. See what 1 John 3:1-2 says; *"Behold, what manner of love the Father hath bestowed upon us, that we should be called the sons of God: therefore the world knoweth us not, because it knew him not. Beloved, now are we the sons of God, and it doth not yet appear what we shall be: but we know that, when he shall appear, we shall be like him; for we shall see him as he is."*

Also in the book of Romans 8:38-39; *For I am persuaded, that neither death, nor life, nor angels, nor principalities, nor power, nor things present, nor things to come, nor height, nor depth, nor any other creature, shall be able to separate us from the love of God, which is in Christ Jesus our Lord.*

Nothing can wrench us from the love of God. God loves you, and He wants you healed!

I read of a doctor who treated a five-year-old boy for an injured eye. The cornea had been slashed by a piece of flying glass. The clear liquid in the front chamber of the eye had drained out, and the iris was protruding from the laceration. So he performed an emergency surgery to reset the iris in its proper position, and a conjunctival flap was carried like a patch over the wound.

A few days later, he removed the dressing from the eye, only to find out that the patch had not held, and the iris was protruding through the cornea again. Then he arranged another surgery for the boy. The boy came back the next day for the surgery, and before he administered the anaesthetic, he made a final examination of the eye. He discovered that the eye was completely healed. There was nothing he could operate on. He was astonished and a little embarrassed. He called the boy's parents, and they told him it was God who healed him. They prayed to God to heal his eyes. The doctor was surprised, and from there, he got the urge to know more about God.

God can heal you; His words can also heal you.

CHAPTER FIVE

DESTROYING THE FEAR OF SICKNESS

There is no fear in love, but perfect love casts out fear. For fear has to do with punishment, and whoever fears has not been perfected in love. 1 John 4:18

The end of fear of sickness is death. It is one thing to recognize the fear of sickness; it is another to discover a remedy for it. One remedy to destroy this fear is the love of God.

There is no greater love than the love of Christ. If Christ had not surrendered Himself to God through the Holy Spirit, to pay the price for man's redemption, God would not have sent Him. But He so loved His Father (God) and the children of His Father (man) that He offered His blood as a sacrifice to redeem man. This is a powerful and undeniable proof of God's love. Love is everything; it conquers fear.

What is love? If you're unsure about what love entails, see what 1 Corinthians 13:4-7 says; *Love endures with patience and serenity, love is kind and thoughtful, and is not jealous or envious; love does not brag and is not proud or arrogant. It is not rude; it is not self-seeking, it is not provoked (nor overly sensitive and easily angered); it does not take into account a wrong endured. It does not rejoice at injustice, but rejoices with the truth (when right and truth prevail). Love bears all things (regardless of what comes), believes all things (looking for the best in each one), hopes all things (remaining steadfast during difficult times), endures all things (without weakening).*

God is love. Whoever lives in love lives in God, and God is in them. There is no fear in love, but perfect love drives out fear because fear has to do with punishment. The one who fears is not made perfect in love.

One way to destroy the spirit of the fear of sickness is through God's mighty love. Look at the children of Israel when Pharaoh refused to let them go to the promised land that God had prepared for them.

Exodus 5:1-7; *And afterward Moses and Aaron went in, and told Pharaoh, Thus saith the LORD God of Israel, Let my people go, that they may hold a feast unto me in the wilderness. And Pharaoh said, who is the LORD, that I should obey his voice to let Israel go? I know not the LORD, neither will I let Israel go. And they said, The God of the Hebrews hath met with us: let us go, we pray thee, three days' journey into the desert, and sacrifice unto the LORD our God; lest he fall upon us with pestilence, or with the sword. And the King of Egypt said unto them, wherefore do ye, Moses and Aaron, let the people from their works? Get you unto your burdens. And Pharaoh said, Behold, the people of the land now are many, and ye make them rest from their burdens. And Pharaoh commanded the same day the taskmasters of the people, and their officers, saying, ye shall no more give the people straw to make brick, as heretofore: let them go and gather straw for themselves.*

Pharaoh refused to let them go and even increased the labour he was subjecting them to. Pharaoh was the fear of sickness that had decided to torment them all their lives. Fear hates to let go of its victims. It fights to stay as if it has found a home in you.

He was the sickness causing the Israelites to fear, but the love of God prevails and He led His children out of the bondage of Pharaoh. So friends, the love of God, your Father, is readily available to set you free from the bondage of fear of sickness.

The story of the Israelites and Pharaoh is enough proof of God's love for His children. Pharaoh refused countless times to let them go, but God was ready to do anything for their freedom. This is one of the greatest love we have seen after the death of Jesus Christ for man's sake.

Why didn't Pharaoh want the Israelites to be free? Because he knew how blessed they were. He used them because they were extraordinary people with great power. How would he let these great people leave his land? This is the same way the fear of sickness doesn't want you to go to the promised land which God has prepared for you. It is a sickness-free life!

The enemy (fear of illness) wants to hinder you from knowing that God has prepared a life in which you will never be sick again, for you. It can be compared to a wealthy man's son living in poverty because he doesn't know his father and, as a result, is unaware of his father's wealth. He is entitled to his father's fortune, but once he realizes who his father is and that he is affluent, he won't have to endure suffering any longer.

So this is what the enemy is trying to do, but your Father's love saturates all of the enemy's devices. Pharaoh detested the people of Israel to the hilt because they were performing significantly better than the Egyptians. He attempted everything to destroy them because he knew they had great strength, making them superior to the Egyptians. The fear of illness also determines how strong God's children are.

This is why he tries to break them from their inner strength. Fear attacks you from the inside, which is your mind, the principal controller of your entire being.

Since the mind controls all actions and makes most of the decisions, fear can easily have complete control over an individual. But God's love is set to break you out of fear!

God's love was so massive that he was ready to kill the firstborn of the Egyptians, including Pharaoh's. He thought God was a joke, but he still refused after God had given the warning about killing his firstborn and the Egyptians' firstborns. His children would not go if He did not. So God proved that He meant business by killing Pharaoh's firstborn for the sake of His children! Exodus 4:22-23; *And thou shalt say unto Pharaoh, Thus saith the Lord, Israel is my son, even my firstborn: and I say unto thee, let my son go, that he may serve me: and if thou refuse to let him go, behold, I will slay thy son, even thy firstborn.*

See what Exodus 11:4-7 says; *And Moses said, Thus saith the LORD, about midnight will I go out into the midst of Egypt: and all the firstborn in the land of Egypt shall die, from the firstborn of Pharaoh that sitteth upon his throne, even unto the firstborn of the maidservant that is behind the mill; and all the firstborn of beasts. And there shall be a great cry throughout all the land of Egypt, such as there was none like it, nor shall be like it any more. But against any of the children of Israel shall not a dog move his tongue, against man or beast: that ye may know how that the LORD doth put a difference between the Egyptians and Israel.*

When a person is in love, a single scratch on that person's skin could make the lover furious, right?

That is the sign of a great lover; a lover loves extremely and can be protective. It can also lead to showing his wrath. God's wrath towards the Egyptians and the King of Egypt was due to the great love He has for His children.

I have a brother whom I adore so much that I would freak out if he has even the tiniest injury. Perhaps the injury was caused by someone attempting to hurt him, I could go mad because of that. I am overly protective of him, and this is born out of the love I have for him. If you love someone, you can't withstand them going through pain and suffering. You can't withstand them being oppressed. I will get angry if I see someone oppressing my brother, not because he is younger but because I love him dearly.

God was so angry that He punished the Egyptians and warned that not a single scratch should be found on the Israelites. This is why He said, *"But against any of the children of Israel shall not a dog move his tongue!"* Friends, God is ready to fight for His children against anything that causes them discomfort. A mere fear of the enemy is not enough to withstand God's love for you.

God heard their cry and saw their discomfort. Imagine how hurt I would be if I see my brother in pain. Then, how much more God when His children are being oppressed?

Fear of sickness is bondage. Cry out to be free from it the way the Israelites cried to be freed. See where God heard his children's cries. Exodus 3:9-12; *Now therefore, behold, the cry of the children of Israel is come unto me: and I have also seen the oppression wherewith the Egyptians oppress them. Come now therefore, and I will send thee unto Pharaoh, that thou mayest bring fort my people the children of the Israel out of Egypt. And Moses said unto God, who am I, that I should go unto Pharaoh, and that I should bring forth the children of Israel out of Egypt? And he said, Certainly I will be with thee; and this shall be a token unto thee, that I have sent thee: When thou hast brought forth the people out of Egypt, ye shall serve God upon this mountain.*

God heard their cry, and He made provision to deliver them out of the hands of the enemy. He heard their groaning and made ways to set them free. This is God's love.

Like Pharaoh, who was unwilling to release God's people, the fear of sickness is difficult to overcome. But the depth of God's love for the Israelites outweighed Pharaoh's depravity. After killing his firstborn child, he was so obstinate that he didn't want to let them go because as the Israelites made their way to the Red Sea, he pursued them.

Let's read Exodus 14:5; *And it was told the king of Egypt that the people fled: and the heart of Pharaoh and of his servants was turned against the people, and they said, Why have we done this, that we have let Israel go from serving us?*

The enemy doesn't let go easily; do you know why? The secret is that once they let go, you will dominate them. Now this is the right way; fear of sickness wouldn't want you to dominate it, because once you are free from it, you will no longer fear it. You will find out the truth and can never be sick. Do you think the enemy wants you to know this secret? This is why he won't let go easily, just like Pharaoh refused to let the children of God go after he had lost his firstborn.

God saw that he was coming after the Israelites towards the red sea, and God said, "Oh, so you are proving you are stubborn? Don't worry, come! I will show you who I am and what I can do to destroy the enemy of my son (the Israelite)!

Pharaoh went after them. Let's read further in Exodus 14:6-12; *And he made ready his chariot, and took his people with him: and he took six hundred chosen chariots, and all the chariots of Egypt, and captains over every one of them. And the LORD hardened the heart of Pharaoh king of Egypt, and he pursued after the children of Israel: and the children of Israel went with an high hand. But the Egyptians pursued after them, all the horses and chariots of Pharaoh, and his horsemen, and his army, and overtook them encamping by the sea, beside Pihahiroth, before Baalzephon.*

And when Pharaoh drew nigh, the children of Israel lifted up their eyes, and, behold, the Egyptians marched after them, and they were sore afraid: and the children of Israel cried out unto the LORD. And they said unto Moses, Because there were no graves in Egypt, hast thou taken us away to die in the wilderness? Wherefore hast thou dealt thus with us, to carry us forth out of Egypt?

Is not this the word that we did tell thee in Egypt, saying Let us alone, that we may serve the Egyptians? For it had been better for us to serve the Egyptians, than that we should die in the wilderness.

When the fear of sickness is too stubborn to leave, you might think you are helpless, but you are not. God is with you, and He will always find a way to deliver you from the hands of fear and heal you in His immense love and mercy.

See Moses' reply to the Israelites in verse 13 of that chapter; *And Moses said unto the people, Fear ye not, stand still, and see the salvation of the LORD, which he will shew to you today: for the Egyptians whom ye have seen today, ye shall see them again no more forever.*

Whatever fear you harbour because of sickness, you shall fear it no more! Because the Lord is said to quench all the fiery darts of the enemy and the love of God will swallow it up in victory. Exodus 14:14: *The LORD shall fight for you, and you shall hold your peace.*

Then God told Moses to use the stick in his hands when they approached the sea. Let me tell you this; God can use anything for the sake of His children. Can you already see the love God has for His children? Can't you feel the gravity of this mighty love?

In verses 15 and 16 of that chapter in Exodus; *And the LORD said unto Moses, Wherefore criest thou unto me? Speak unto the children of Israel, that they go forward: but lift thou up thy rod, and stretch out thine hand over the sea, and divide it: and the children of Israel shall go on dry ground through the midst of the sea.*

Sorry to cut the flow between the verses. But if you do not trust God to heal you before, this chapter should give you proof that God can do anything for your sake. Can you imagine splitting a sea for His children to pass on dry ground? What is that sickness that God cannot heal? What is that Pharaoh that has refused to let you go? Ask yourself: can that sickness withstand God's love and power?

We shall read further from verses 17-25; *And I, behold, I will harden the hearts of the Egyptians, and they shall follow them: and I will get me honour upon Pharaoh, and upon all his host, upon his chariots, and upon his horsemen. And the Egyptians shall know that I am the LORD, when I have gotten me honour upon Pharaoh, upon his chariots, and upon his horsemen. And the angel of God, which went before the camp of Israel, removed and went behind them; and the pillar of the cloud went from before their face, and stood behind them.*

And it came between the camp of the Egyptians and the camp of Israel; and it was a cloud and darkness to them, but it gave light by night to these: so that the one came not near the other all the night. And Moses stretched out his hand over the sea; and the LORD caused the sea to go back by a strong east wind all that night, and made the sea dry land, and the waters were divided.

And the children of Israel went into the midst of the sea upon the dry ground: and the waters were a wall unto them on their right hand, and on their left. And the Egyptians pursued, and went in after them to the midst of the sea, even all Pharaoh's horses, his chariots, and his horsemen. And it came to pass, that in the morning watch the LORD looked unto the host of the Egyptians through the pillar of fire and of the cloud, and troubled the host of the Egyptians.

And took off the chariot wheels, that they drove them heavily: so that the Egyptians said, Let us flee from the face of Israel; for the LORD fighteth for them against the Egyptians.

When the adversary has done everything in their power to keep you from leaving, they will finally give up, but it might be too late, for the Lord's wrath will swallow them up!

We go further from verses 26-30; *And the LORD said unto Moses, Stretch out thine hand over the sea, that the waters may come again upon the Egyptians, upon their chariots, and upon their horsemen. And Moses stretched forth his hand over the sea, and the sea returned to his strength when the morning appeared, and the Egyptians fled against it, and the LORD overthrew the Egyptians in the midst of the sea. And the waters returned, and covered the chariots and the horsemen, and all the host of Pharaoh that came into the sea after them; there remained not so much as one of them. But the children of Israel walked upon dry land in the midst of the sea; and the waters were a wall unto them on their right hand and on their left. Thus, the LORD saved Israel that day out of the hand of the Egyptians; and Israel saw the Egyptians dead upon the sea shore.*

God never accepts defeat. If the fear of sickness is too stubborn to let you go, God's love will defeat it right now!

Know that God's love is sufficient for you, so you should eradicate every fear. God is love and He loves you. Therefore, there should be no room for the fear of sickness in your life or concerning your health. Because His healing power is about to hit you right now through the Holy Spirit in Jesus' name!

The love of God renews you to fight the fear of sickness. God cannot work with fear; He works with your faith. The love of God boosts your faith and helps you trust in Him. The love of God stirs up your faith.

1 John 4:18-19; *There is no fear in love; but perfect love casteth out fear: because fear hath torment. He that feareth is not made perfect in love. We love him, because he first loved us.*

When you think of God's love for you, you will have nothing to fear. You cannot have the fear of sickness or be afraid when in a hospital bed. When you understand the power of God's love and that God truly loves you, you will no longer be afraid of dying, falling sick, or getting infected by some viruses or diseases. If you could only truly comprehend the depth of God's love, you will have nothing to fear.

You should be reminded that nothing—not even your sin—can separate us from the love of God. Do you know that God overlooked our sins and still loved us by letting His begotten son die for us on the cross? Romans 5:8-11; *But God commendeth his love towards us, in that, while we were yet sinners, Christ died for us. Much more then, being now justified by his blood, we shall be saved from wrath through him. For if, when we were enemies, we were reconciled to God by the death of his Son, much more, being reconciled, we shall be saved by his life. And not only so, but we also joy in God through our LORD Jesus Christ, by whom we have now received the atonement.*

Therefore, friends, nothing can separate us from the love of God, not even the creepy, lying fear, not even that damn sickness. Romans 8:35-39 says; *Who shall separate us from the love of Christ? Shall tribulation, or distress, or persecution, or famine, or nakedness, or peril, or sword? As it is written, For thy sake we are killed all the day long; we are accounted as sheep for the slaughter. Nay, in all these things we are more than conquerors through him that loved us. For I am persuaded, that neither death, nor life, nor angels, nor principalities, nor powers, nor things present, nor things to come, nor height, nor depth, nor any other creature, shall be able to separate us from the love of God, which is in Christ Jesus our Lord.*

If God is more powerful than anything in heaven and on earth, how much more is the sickness refusing to let you go? There is nothing powerful enough to separate us from God's love. Not even Pharaoh was powerful enough to separate the Israelites from God's love.

God's love is too massive to comprehend. This is why we should fear nothing except Him. Ephesian 3:17-19; *That Christ may dwell in your hearts by faith; that ye, being rooted and grounded in love, may be able to comprehend with all saints what is the breadth, and length, and depth, and height; and to know the love of Christ, which passeth knowledge, that ye might be filled with all the fullness of God.*

The love of God surpasses all things. Therefore, instead of getting scared of sickness or being afraid during illness, why not turn to God to shield you and keep you safe? See what Psalm 5:11–12 says; *But let all those that put their trust in thee rejoice: Let them ever shout for joy, because thou defendest them: let them also that love thy name be joyful in thee. For thou, LORD, wilt bless the righteous; with favour wilt thou compass him as with a shield.*

When you choose to trust God rather than being fearful, you have defeated the devil. He will put His shield and tender, loving kindness (massive love) around you to heal you. God also heals with love and mercy through His Holy Spirit.

His Word of Truth

Peace I leave with you, my peace I give unto you: not as the world giveth, give I unto you. Let not your heart be troubled, neither let it be afraid. John 14:27.

The word of God gives you peace in times of trouble or fear. When the spirit of fear comes to scare you, the word of God is the remedy to get you back on your feet. God didn't say there wouldn't be tribulation or temptation, but He had made provision for you to overcome that tribulation. John 16:33; *"These things I have spoken unto you, that in me ye might have peace.*

In the world ye shall have tribulation: but be of good cheer; I have overcome the world.

Jesus Christ is a perfect example of someone who faced many tribulations. When He wanted to perform a miracle, He turned to the Father for instructions. This is why He said, "I can do nothing on my own except by the Father." See in John 5:30-33; *I can of my own self do nothing: as I hear, I judge: and my judgement is just; because I seek not mine own will, but the will of the Father which hath sent me. If I bear witness of myself, my witness is not true. There is another that beareth witness of me; and I know that the witness which he witnesseth of me is true. Ye sent unto John, and he bare witness unto the truth.*

He always sought His Father's word whenever He didn't know what to do. Jesus has given us the perfect example, to always go through the word of God in times of tribulation. God's word is the solution to any fear you may have. His words will give you the boldness to get rid of that fear. His words will guide you on what to do.

Also, when Gideon was afraid, the Lord told him not to be afraid, and that he would have peace. Judge 6:22-23; *And when Gideon perceived that he was the angel of the LORD. Gideon said, Alas, O Lord God! for I have seen the angel of the Lord face to face. And the LORD said to him, "Peace be with you; do not fear, you shall not die."*

Gideon was quite terrified of the assignment he was given, but he relied on God's word, and the Spirit of God descended on Gideon.

Whenever adversity arises, you will be at a loss for what to do, especially if sickness, agony, or terror stops you from thinking about God's words. Nonetheless, the moment you realize that God's words offer answers to every problem, you will be delivered.

The word of God is mighty. This is what Hebrews 4:12 says about the word of God. *"For the word of God is quick, and powerful, and sharper than any two-edged sword, piercing even to the dividing asunder of soul and spirit, and of the joints and marrow, and is a discerner of the thoughts and intents of heart."* The word of God has the solution to all things, including fear of sickness, sickness itself, anxiety, diseases, etc. It is like a master key that opens all doors. The word of God is powerful enough to penetrate your bones. How then can sickness torment your body or fear take control of your heart? His words can heal. They are capable of making the thoughts of man right.

Whenever fear comes to your mind, read the word of God. You remember I said, fear is one of the strongest weapons of the enemy. You need God's words to defeat it. Psalm 27:1-4 says; *The LORD is my light and my salvation; whom shall I fear? The LORD is the strength*

The word of God is what you go back to in times of fear and tribulation.

Here is the story of a man who had cancer and thought that his days were over. I read this story from one of Kathryn Kuhlman's books. He was diagnosed with lymphoma, and it got worse daily. He winced in pain every five minutes, whenever he tried to walk.

He was in great agony that he cried in secret because he wouldn't want his wife more depressed about his situation than she already is. Crying in secret was the best option for him, and it was dreadful for a grown man to cry. But this was a real pain—the kind of pain you would rather die than experience.

Since he thought he would be dying soon, he wanted to say goodbye to his only daughter, who was already married and lived in a different city. His wife drove him to her house the next day, where he was to spend the night and leave the following day, in the evening.

His daughter cried when she saw him. She didn't believe it was the last time she would be seeing her Dad because she was a Christian and believed God would heal him. They cried and prayed, then went to bed.

The next day, he locked himself in his room. His daughter came to call him for breakfast, but he said he was fasting, and that was on a Sunday morning. She was surprised to hear that he was fasting in his condition, and she asked him why he was doing that. His reply was, "I saw this in the Bible; that God answers your prayer faster when you fast and pray."

She was amazed and left him alone to do what he had discovered from the word of God. He didn't eat breakfast and went to church that morning. Would you believe that when he returned from church, he could no longer feel those terrible pains anymore and signs of cancer had disappeared? There! He knew the healing power of God had touched him.

In this story, his situation was worse and he thought he was going to die, but despite that, he still went to God's word to search for a solution instead of allowing fear to dominate him. As Christians, we don't accept defeat so easily. We go back to our Father's word to renew our minds with the help of the Holy Spirit (God's Spirit).

Just as the word of God helped Jesus, Gideon, and many others who were sick, it will help you too; all you need to do is rely on His words and remember that He loves you dearly. He loves you, beloved; therefore, do not be afraid because you have God backing you in every breath you take.

Psalm 19: 1-14 *"He that dwelleth in the secret place of the most High shall abide under the shadow of the Almighty. I will say of the LORD, He is my refuge and my fortress: my God, in him will I trust. Surely he shall deliver thee from the snare of the fowler, and from the noisome pestilence. He shall cover thee with his feathers, and under his wings shalt thou trust: his truth shall be thy shield and buckler.*

Thou shalt not be afraid for the terror by night; nor the arrow that flieth by day; Nor for the pestilence that walketh in darkness; nor for the destruction that wasteth at noonday. A thousand shall fall at thy side, and ten thousand at thy right hand; but it shall not come nigh thee. Only with thine eyes shalt thou behold, and see the reward of the wicked. Because thou hast made the LORD, which is my refuge, Even the most High, thy habitation.

There shall no evil befall thee, neither shall any plague come nigh thy dwelling. For he shall give his angels charge over thee, to keep thee in all thy ways. They shall bear thee up in their hands, lest thou dash thy foot against a stone. Thou shall tread upon the lion and adder: the young lion and the dragon shalt thou trample under feet. Because he hath set his love upon me, therefore will I deliver him: I will set him on high, because he hath known my name."

This is God's word to you; have no fear!

Give Him Praise

Another thing that destroys fear is praise. Give God praise instead of being scared. When you praise God, it earns you His mighty presence, and when God's presence is with you, nothing in this world can withstand it.

Remember, you are of God and not of the world, so you have the power and a greater chance of victory over the things of this world that try to torment or oppress you. Like David, who gave God lots of praise when he had battles to fight. Psalm 144:1-2; *"Praise be to the LORD my rock, who trains my hands for war, my fingers for battle. He is my loving God and my fortress, my stronghold and my deliverer, my shield, in whom I take refuge, who subdues peoples under me."*

One of David's secret warfare is praising God. His opponent would spend time preparing for battle while David is in his prayer room, singing praises to God. By this, he earned God's heart and blessings, and His spirit fell upon David, giving him the supernatural strength to fight the war and emerge the winner. Psalms 16:11; *Thou wilt shew me the path of life: in thy presence is fullness of joy; at thy right hand there are pleasures for evermore.*

When there's God's presence with you, no fear and sickness can come near you. In the presence of God, there is fullness of joy. When you are full of joy, what permits fear to control your mind? What gives the enemy access to oppress you? Nothing!

Praising God moves Him to bless you from His throne. When you praise God, He comes down to receive it. It is the only thing that moves God from His throne down to where the praise is taking place. My friends and I had this experience when we began to give God intense praise and worship. That was my first time of hearing God speak. He came down; I will never forget that experience.

This is why the enemy was never able to defeat David. He always felt God's presence because every second of his life, he gave God praise. See what Psalm 34:1-6 says; *"I will bless the LORD at all times: his praise shall continually be in my mouth. My soul shall make her boast in the LORD: the humble shall hear thereof, and be glad. O magnify the LORD with me, and let us exalt his name together. I sought the LORD, and he heard me, and delivered me from all my fears. They looked unto him, and were lightened: and their faces were not ashamed. This poor man cried and the LORD heard him, and saved him out of all his troubles."*

There is no fear, no pain, no disease, and no sense of defeat in God's presence.

One of my uncles experienced something, perhaps a spiritual attack.

He was coming back from his workplace. When he got to the pedestrian crossing across the highway, a young girl grabbed his left hand, pleading with him to take her through as well.

He agreed and allowed the young girl to hold his left hand firmly. They crossed successfully, but she abruptly left him and ran away. He was perplexed at how she left and felt strange, but he pushed the thoughts aside as he made his way home.

As soon as he arrived at his house, he started experiencing discomfort in his left hand, and all of a sudden, he was unable to move it. It appeared as though the hand had stopped functioning or that there were no longer any living cells there.

Friends, that was the time he should have allowed fear to enter his mind. There were reasons to be afraid in that situation because, come to think of it, a young girl was holding him and he suddenly lost feeling in his hands. Wasn't that a big problem to begin with?

But no, he didn't freak out, neither was he afraid!

He refused to surrender to Satan because he knew that his heavenly Father is a powerful healer. Despite having a lot of discomfort and difficulties lying down, he was calm. He started praising God while rolling wildly on the bed.

While praising God, he slept off. He dreamed of Jesus operating on the hand while he slept. When he woke up, his left hand now had life; it was no longer dead, and the pains were gone.

This is what giving praise to God can do. Every devilish attack is destroyed by His presence. His presence brings healing. You have nothing to be afraid of in His presence. Psalm 148:13-14; *Let them praise the name of the LORD: for his name alone is excellent; his glory is above the earth and heaven. He also exalteth the horn of his people, the praise of all his saints; even of the*

children of Israel, a people near unto him. Praise ye the
LORD.

You can be delivered from the attack of sickness by praising God. Here is one of my stories: as soon as I got off the bus on my way to the hostel, suddenly, I became sick. It was a cold I had never had before. The moment I stepped outside, it started to rain, and the situation got worse. I began to shiver and quake. I tried to manage it but was unable to.

When I got into another vehicle to get to the bus stop, the cold got worse. My teeth started to chatter, and no matter what I tried, it wasn't getting any better. I felt as though I was going to die. But the truth is I cannot die but live to proclaim the works of the Lord.

When I arrived at my hostel, it was becoming more serious. I could not stand or move my legs as my entire body started to quiver. I finally made it to my room and lay down on the bed since I couldn't stand any longer due to excruciating leg pain. I was unaware that it was an attack until the Holy Spirit spoke to me and told me to stand up.

Even though I was unable to stand on my two feet, I didn't protest because I could hear the voice of the Holy Spirit. He ordered me to sing praises to God after I managed to stand up.

I followed the orders and started praising God. When I began to walk unintentionally around while offering God praise, I felt stronger and the pain in my leg started to lessen. Then I started to warm up! I started sweating in the middle of singing, and it took me off guard because I had given up hope of surviving the cold.

I doubled my praises to God when I noticed that I was getting better, and that evening, I was completely healed and released from the devil's attack.

CHAPTER SIX

SICKNESS IS A SPIRIT

In the beginning, it was not so. God didn't create you with sickness; it was never so at the beginning of man's creation.

And they came over unto the other side of the sea, into the country of the Gadarenes. And when he was come out of the ship, immediately there met him out of the tombs a man with an unclean spirit, who had his dwelling among the tombs; and no man could bind him, no, not with chains: because that he had been often bound with fetters and chains, and the chains had been plucked asunder by him, and the fetters broken in pieces: neither could any man tame him. And always, night and day, he was in the mountains, and in the tombs, crying, and cutting himself with stones. Mark 5:1-5.

Sickness has always been a spirit, just as fear is a spirit. They are spirits from the devil, sent out from hell to torment the children of God and put them into slavery; to make them miserable, to make them curse God, and to make them suffer excruciating pains. This has been his mandate from the beginning, but the great healer is set to free you from that spirit of sickness today.

Someone is sick, and people think it is normal. How would that be normal? How can a headache be normal? Yes, there is a spirit behind headaches too! You think it's normal, which is why it continues to torment you. I have seen someone die from a headache, and you still think it's normal?

How can it be normal for someone to cut himself with a stone and cry all day and night? This is the torture of the evil spirit!

There is a spirit behind anything ungodly, and sickness is never godly. God never planned for you to be sick, and He never intended for any of His children to die through sickness. Every action is always motivated by a spirit. Whatever the sickness is; there is a spirit behind it. There is a spirit behind the insanity, prostitution, deception, headaches, cancer, and diabetes, among several others. There is a spirit at work within. Moreover, the most powerful spirit in the universe supports everything godly. It is the Holy Spirit of God.

Whereas the spirit that is not of God does the opposite, the spirit that is of God possesses you to act morally and under God's will, which causes your life to blossom like a tree planted by the river. You are directed by the Spirit of God to live uprightly.

See what Psalm 1:3- 4 says; *And he shall be like a tree planted by the rivers of water, that bringeth forth his fruit in his season; His leaf also shall not wither; And whatsoever he doeth shall prosper. The ungodly are not so: But are like the chaff which the wind driveth away.* This is what the Spirit of God leads a man into, while the spirit of the devil leads to the destruction of man.

Dedicating your mind to any act is submitting yourself to the spirit behind that act. So, if you dedicate yourself to treating sicknesses all the time, you are unknowingly submitting yourself to the devil through the spirit responsible for that sickness.

The devil is not a joke. Do you think he will let the children of God be at peace when he knows he has already been defeated by the son of God, who has raised us above him? Of course, he will put up a fight as a loser! And losers are always ready for a war they know they cannot win.

You need to be awake in your spirit as a child of God. You must use discernment. Children of God should be able to tell what belongs to God and what doesn't. 1 Thessalonians 5:21 *"But test everything; hold fast what is good."* 1 Corinthians 2:10-12 *"But God hath revealed them unto us by his Spirit: for the Spirit searcheth all things, yea, the deep things of God. For what man knoweth the things of a man, save the spirit of man which is in him? Even so the things of God knoweth no man, but the Spirit of God. Now we have received, not the spirit of the world, but the spirit which is of God; that we might know the things that are freely given to us of God."*

Don't say it is normal when someone starts falling ill. No sickness is normal. You are of God; therefore, you should discern that.

Sickness is a spirit, and Jesus called it an unclean spirit, a demonic spirit. Luke 13:10–13: *And he was teaching in one of the synagogues on the sabbath. And, behold, there was a woman which had a spirit of infirmity eighteen years, and was bowed together, and could in no wise lift up herself. And when Jesus saw her, he called her to him, and said unto her, Woman, thou art loosed from the infirmity. And he laid his hands on her and immediately she was made straight, and glorified God.*

You can imagine the shape the spirit of sickness moulded her into, disfiguring her and making her a cripple. Thank God for Jesus, the Son of God who came to rescue us from the oppression of the devil. It was too much!

The same unclean spirit made someone deaf and dumb in the Bible. If you see someone who is blind, dumb or deaf, there is a spirit behind it. The aim of the devil is for a man not to glorify God, and man can only glorify God with his body.

The body is the temple of the Lord. However, how can a man honour God without his eyes if he loses his sight? How can he worship God if he is deaf? How can he convince those who have deaf ears? And if he is blind, how can he see the people he ought to bring to God? And if he is dumb, how does he speak out God's words to people? How can he save the lost souls? Therefore, it is the ultimate plan of the devil for a man not to glorify God. He attacks the body, which is the temple of the most High.

Here is the scripture; Mark 9:25-27 *"When Jesus saw that the people came running together, he rebuked the foul spirit, saying unto him, Thou dumb and deaf spirit, I charge thee, come out of him, and enter no more into him. And the spirit cried, rent him sore, and came out of him: and he was as one dead; insomuch that many said, He is dead. But Jesus took him by the hand, and lifted him up; and he arose."*

Those ungodly spirits control men to do the opposite of God's will. It is like turning man against God to do the things He detests. Someone was delivered from a deceitful spirit, which is also known as a serpent spirit. This spirit made that person deceitful, and you know how God detests lies. This is what the evil spirit of Satan does, to make a man do the things God hates.

Consider the carnival that took place in Brazil. My heart ached as I watched that movie, seeing how Satan had moved their hearts away from God's will. It was horrible to see how thoroughly they had been immersed in the spirit of Satan. They were used by the evil spirit within them to mock God, who is their very creator and Father. Satan would be ecstatic at that point since it gives him tremendous joy, to see God's children act in opposition to His will. Satan is excited when children of God disobey Him.

They were taken over by the demonic spirit of Satan and started making statues and images of the devil. They started to adore the devil. Do you think they were doing this in their right mind? No! Satan has influenced them with his evil spirits, and he has taken over their minds and senses. It is also their fault because they permitted him; this is something they might be unaware of.

I'll explain how people can allow Satan to influence their lives. They are initially attracted to the items they see; they buy and start using them. Unknowingly, this lures the spirit of Satan.

I will share a story with you. Earlier, I said someone was delivered from a serpent spirit. You might want to know how that spirit was able to possess her. It was from a waist bead she purchased with her money. Also, someone had been possessed through a cloth that looked like snakeskin. This is how people invite evil spirits unknowingly into their life. The devil's spirit is no different.

Nothing on earth could have compelled them (in Brazil) to mock God and engage in those diabolical deeds if they had been possessed by the Spirit of God. But as usual, Satan's spirit is simply motivated by a desire to see God's creation destroyed; therefore, let God's creatures disobey Him. Satan wants us to rebel against God, as he did when he was an angel in heaven with God.

Satan is a liar, and a filthy, unclean spirit. The spirit of sickness caged a woman for complete eight years. See oppression! Luke 13:16; *And ought not this woman, being a daughter of Abraham, whom Satan hath bound, lo, these eighteen years, be loosed from this bond on the sabbath day?*

Let's read the complete scripture from verse 11 to see how Jesus set her free.

Luke 13:11-17; *And, behold, there was a woman which had a spirit of infirmity eighteen years, and was bowed together, and could in no wise lift up herself. And when Jesus saw her, he called her to him, and said unto her, woman, thou art loosed from the infirmity. And he laid his hands on her: and immediately she was made straight, and glorified God. And the ruler of the synagogue answered with indignation, because that Jesus had healed on the sabbath day, and said unto the people, There are six days in which men ought to work: in them therefore come and be healed, and not on the sabbath day.*

The Lord then answered him, and said, thou hypocrite, doth not each one of you on the sabbath loose his ox or his ass from the stall, and lead him away to watering? And ought not this woman, being a daughter of Abraham, whom satan hath bound, lo, these eighteen years, be loosed from this bond on the sabbath day? And when he had said these things, all his adversaries were ashamed: and all the people rejoiced for all the glorious that were done by him.

The woman, who had been crippled for 18 years, was immediately healed by the touch of Jesus. The devil never likes it when we are set free from his oppression. You can see the rulers wanted to make an offence out of it, for healing the woman on the sabbath day. Meanwhile, they had all been doing one activity or another on the same sabbath day. But when it came to healing the woman, they wanted to create a problem out of it. The devil creates enemies for Jesus to stop His good work and heal people who were sick and oppressed.

Jesus has all authority; therefore, He spoke and exposed the things they do in secret on the sabbath day, and they were ashamed. The devil suffered defeat again, and glory was given to God most High.

The devil is wicked. No wonder Jesus said he is here for destruction. How can he put someone in bondage for 18 years? And also afflict a man to make him start cutting himself with stone? What a demonic spirit! A spirit of insanity!

Whatever the spirit is, Jesus has the authority, which is why they obey him. Let's look into Matthew 8:16-17, where He cast out the spirit with a word and healed all who were sick. *"When the even was come, they brought unto him many that were possessed with devils: and cast out the spirits with his word, and healed all that were sick: that it might be fulfilled which was spoken by Esaias the prophet, saying, Himself took our infirmities, and bare our sicknesses."*

He healed all who were sick and cast out the foul spirit of the devil.

See how Jesus defeated the spirit oppressing the man whose habitat was the tombs and who couldn't be chained because the spirit that had possessed him was stronger. *"And when he was come out of the ship, immediately there met him out of the tombs a man with an unclean spirit, who had his dwelling among the tombs; and no man could bind him, no, not with chains: because that he had been often bound with fetters and chains, and the chains had been plucked asunder by him, and the fetters broken in pieces: neither could any man tame him. And always, night and day, he was in the mountains, and in the tombs, crying, and cutting himself with stones.*

But when he saw Jesus afar off, he ran and worshiped him, and cried with a loud voice, and said, What have I to do with thee, Jesus, thou Son of the most high God? I adjure thee by God, that thou torment me not. For he said unto him, Come out of the man, thou unclean spirit. And he asked him, What is thy name? And he answered, saying, My name is Legion: for we are many. And he besought him much that he would not send them away out of the country.

Now there was there nigh unto the mountains a great herd of swine feeding. And all the devils besought him, saying, send us into the swine, that we may enter into them. And forthwith Jesus gave them leave. And the unclean spirits went out, and entered into the swine: and the herd ran violently down a steep place into the sea, (they were about two thousand); and were choked in the sea. Mark 5:2-13.

Jesus has power over evil spirits. Those people fear Jesus. From the Bible, we can see how he hurried to Jesus and begged him not to cast him out of the man's body. And to think they have names! When I read that the spirit's name was Legion, I laughed out loud.

Evil spirits are continually on the move, looking for victims to dominate and live in. As they are banished from one body, they look for another one that is unoccupied to stay. This is why it is wrong for you to be near a deliverance session if you aren't praying because the vexed spirit can leave that body and enter another.

Prayer prevents the spirit from invading because the environment would be too hot for him to stay.

Jesus defeats Satan so that God may be praised. They were shocked when Jesus cast out the spirit that was controlling the people at the synagogue because they had never seen anything like it. Read Matthew 9:32–35.

As they went out, behold, they brought to him a dumb man possessed with a devil. And when the devil was cast out, the dumb spake: and the multitudes marvelled, saying, it was never so seen in Israel. But the Pharisees said, he casteth out the devils through the prince of the devils. And Jesus went about all the cities and villages, teaching in their synagogues, and preaching the gospel of the kingdom, healing every sickness and every disease among the people.

The Spirit of God had anointed the Son of God to cast out demons and heal everyone who is under the influence of the devil. This is why sickness is never God's will because He anointed His son to heal the sick. Acts 10:38 *"How God anointed Jesus of Nazareth with the Holy Ghost and with power: who went about doing good, and healing all that were oppressed of the devil; for God was with him."*

Jesus has all authority and Satan knows that. He is like a roaring lion with no power. The Son of God has defeated him, and only He can heal and cast out the spirit of sickness. He, therefore, gave us the blueprint for casting out the spirit of sickness; His name. Mark 16:17; *And these signs shall follow them that believe; in my name shall they cast out devils; they shall speak with new tongues.*

So friends, since Jesus has defeated the devil and cast out all evil spirits, He gave us His name to cast out the spirit of sickness. The name of Jesus carries authority;

when you feel any symptoms of sickness, cast it out in the name of Jesus, and it shall flee.

Here is a secret: all demons are scared of the name 'Jesus'. Once you call the name with authority and faith, demons become scared. I was with my friends one night, and we prayed until dawn. The meeting was not only for prayers; we also gathered to discuss Christ.

While we were praying on that field, we could feel evil powers there. Suddenly, I got a rhema from the Holy Spirit saying, 'Jesus is Lord'. I heard it. Then He gave further understanding, saying, "Do you know what the LORD is? LORD is the overall king. LORD is someone whom everybody fears (humans, demons, spirits, etc.). Now know that Jesus is LORD." I screamed it out to my friends and told them the explanation (deep mysteries) the Holy Spirit gave me about 'Jesus is LORD'. Then they began to say it out as they meant it in their hearts. "JESUS CHRIST IS LORD!"

We began to feel the demons stepping back and drifting far away from us. One of them sees things, and he saw the demons drifting back from that field.

Therefore, friends, there's power in the name of Jesus. Believe it, and it will work for you. Jesus has given us the authority in His name to cast out the spirit of sickness, and it works. I heard about my friends who went for evangelism, preaching to people about Christ. They encountered a sick person.

He crumbled on the bed, and could barely rise on his own. They saw how sick he was, and then they preached to him about Christ and how He died for his sake. The man listened to them and nodded his head repeatedly.

When they were done preaching, they decided to pray for him. They believe sickness has no power over the children of God. They prayed and began to cast out the spirit of the sickness in him using the name of Jesus.

The spirit was out and the man was healed.

Friends, this also happened because they had faith in the name of Jesus Christ. They have faith that it will work for them. If they had not had faith in the name of Jesus, they would be wasting their time there.

See what happened in Mark 9:14-20; *And when he came to his disciples, he saw a great multitude about them, and the scribes questioning with them. And straightway all the people, when they beheld him, were greatly amazed, running to him saluted him. And he asked the scribes, what question ye with them?*

And one of the multitude answered and said, Master, I have brought unto thee my son, which hath a dumb spirit; and wheresoever he taketh him, he teareth him: and he foameth, and gnashed with his teeth, and pineth away: and I spake to thy disciples that they should cast him out; and they could not.

He answered him, and saith, O faithless generation, how long shall I be with you? How long shall I suffer you? Bring him unto me. And they brought him unto him: and when he saw him, straightway the spirit tare him; and he fell on the ground, and wallowed foaming.

The disciples were not able to cast out the spirit of dumbness from the young boy because of their lack of faith. Then Jesus asked them, "Oh faithless generation, how long will you continue like this?"

If you want to cast out the spirit of sickness, you need to apply faith, using the name of Jesus. For we wrestle not against the flesh. Ephesians 6:10-17; *Finally, my brethren, be strong in the Lord, and in the power of his might. Put on the whole armour of God, that ye may be able to stand against the wiles of the devil. For we wrestle not against flesh and blood, but against principalities, against powers, against the rulers of the darkness of the world, against spiritual wickedness in high places. Wherefore take unto you the whole armour of God, that ye may be able to withstand in the evil day, and having done all, to stand.*

Stand therefore, having your loins girt about with truth, and having on the breastplate of righteousness; and your feet shod with the preparation of the gospel of peace; above all, taking the shield of faith, wherewith ye shall be able to quench all the fiery darts of the wicked. And take the helmet of salvation, and the sword of the Spirit, which is the word of God.

Even God has said we should take up the shield of faith in all situations to quench all the fiery darts of the enemy! Finally, brethren, no spirit of sickness has the power to torment us. See in John 19:30; *When Jesus had received the sour wine, he said, 'it is finished', and he bowed his head and gave up his spirit.*

Jesus gave up the ghost when He had taken all bitterness, including sickness, for man's sake. Then He rose by the power of the Holy Spirit, which quickened His body. Friends, that power that quickened His body is in you. The power has quickened your mortal body; therefore, you cannot be sick.

Jesus said it was finished!

CHAPTER SEVEN

I AM THE LORD WHO HEALS

And said, if thou wilt diligently hearken to the voice of the LORD thy God, and wilt do that which is right in his sight, and wilt give ear to his commandments, and keep all his statues, I will put none of these diseases upon thee, which I have brought upon the Egyptians: for I am the LORD that healeth thee. Exodus 15:26

This Bible verse gave birth to this book through the Holy Spirit. Jesus is our great physician, and His power, knowledge, and abilities are without limitations because He is Jehovah-Rapha, our God who heals.

Healing is one of the greatest ways in which souls can be brought to Christ. It is the fastest way to convince people about God. God doesn't say something without giving you proof because He knows without it, men will turn Him down out of ignorance.

Jesus truly heals. There are so many places in the Bible where people became healed through Jesus Christ. The sweetest part is that it is still the same today. You can get healed and as a believer, it is your right to be healed.

Jesus healed two blind men. There's no case that God cannot settle. See what happened in Matthew 20:30-34; *And, behold, two blind men sitting by the way side, when they heard that Jesus passed by, cried out, saying, Have mercy on us, O Lord, thou Son of David. And the multitude rebuked them, because they should hold their peace: but they cried the more, saying, Have mercy on us, O Lord, thou Son of David.*

And Jesus stood still, and called them, and said, What will ye that I shall do unto you? They say unto him, Lord, that our eyes may be opened. So Jesus had compassion on them, and touched their eyes: and immediately their eyes received sight, and they followed him.

The great physician is here to heal you now! God says, "There's nothing too hard for me" in Jeremiah 32:27; *Behold, I am the LORD, the God of all flesh: is there anything too hard for me?* Is it not time to cry out to God about that sickness? Whatever the sickness is, it is not too hard for God.

Cancer, spinal injury, broken legs, blindness, diabetes, stroke, diseases of the heart and liver, lung problems, infection, asthma, diarrhoea, fibroids, tuberculosis, and appendicitis cannot withstand God. No disease, no sickness, can withstand God.

Whatever the sickness is, it is time. Cry out to the great healer and proclaim your healing now because you are of God.

See where Jesus healed a great multitude in Matthew 15:29-31; *And Jesus departed from thence, and came nigh unto the sea of Galilee; and went up into a mountain, and sat down there. And great multitudes came unto him, having with them those that were lame, blind, dumb, maimed, and many others, and cast them down at Jesus' feet; and he healed them: insomuch that the multitude wondered, when they saw the dumb to speak, the maimed to be whole, the lame to walk, and the blind to see: and they glorified the God of Israel.*

In verse 30, you can see 'many others' was mentioned there. It means many with various sicknesses and diseases came, and Jesus healed them. Now, what is stopping you from coming to the great healer? Come now and be healed; your time is now! Cry out to Jesus.

It is your time to touch Jesus. It is your time to tap into the healing virtues of Jesus. Just as many touched him and were made whole in Matthew 14:34-36; *And when they were gone over, they came into the land of Gennesaret. And when the men of that place had knowledge of him, they sent out into all that country round about, and brought unto him all that were diseased; and besought him that they might only touch the hem of his garment: and as many as touched were made perfectly whole.*

Today, Jesus must not pass you by. Tap into His healing virtue and be healed. Claim it by faith!

There is no sickness that Jesus cannot heal. Jesus can give life to dead bones. Ezekiel 37:1-6; *The hand of the LORD was upon me, and carried me out in the spirit of the LORD, and set me down in the midst of the valley which was full of bones, and caused me to pass by them round about: and behold, there were very many in the open valley; and lo, they were very dry. And he said unto me, Son of man, can these bones live? And I answered, O Lord GOD, thou knowest.*

Again he said unto me, Prophesy upon these bones, and say unto them, O ye dry bones, hear the word of the LORD. Thus saith the Lord God unto these bones; behold I will cause breath to enter into you, and ye shall live: and I will lay sinews upon you, and will bring up flesh upon you, and cover you with skin, and put breath in you, and ye shall live; and ye shall know that I am the LORD.

Now tell that sickness to hear the word of the Lord — that you are completely healed! The word of the Lord is quick, sharp, and powerful, sharper than any two-edged sword. Therefore, the word of the Lord is healing your body, bones, and internal organs from any sickness today!

See the man with the withered (dry or dead) hand that Jesus healed in the bible. Matthew 12:9-13; *And when he was departed thence, he went into their synagogue: and behold, there was a man which had his hand withered. And they asked him, saying, is it lawful to heal on the sabbath days? That they might accuse him. And he said unto them, what man shall there be among you, that shall have one sheep, and if it fall into a pit on the sabbath day, will he not lay hold on it and lift it out?*

How much then is a man better than a sheep? Wherefore it is lawful to do well on the sabbath days. The saith he to the man, stretch forth thine hand. And he stretched it forth; and it was restored whole, like as the other.

There is nothing my God cannot do! He healed these people in the Bible; He still heals today. God is healing people every day. He is the same yesterday, today, and forever (Hebrews 13:8), and what Jesus says to one, He says to all. The healing He performs for one, He can perform for all.

I will show you ways through which God heals:

1. Through the Name of Jesus

I have been mentioning the name of Jesus in every prayer since the introduction of this book. Why? Because that name is precious, powerful, and mighty. Even the devil knows it, and that is why he bows at the mention of this mighty name.

You can be healed through the name of Jesus. The name of Jesus is not just something to be praised. It is also a key given to us to heal sickness and diseases. We not only give thanks to the name; we also receive healing through the name.

See what Jesus says in Mark 16:17-18; *And these signs shall follow them that believe; in my name shall they cast out devils, they shall speak with new tongues; they shall take up serpents; and if they drink any deadly thing, it shall not hurt them; they shall lay hands on the sick, and they shall recover.*

He has commanded us to use His name. God has given all authority to Jesus, and nothing can withstand His name when mentioned with faith and authority. Philippians 2:10; *that at the name of Jesus every knee should bow, of things in heaven, and things in earth, and things under earth; and that every tongue should confess that Jesus Christ is Lord, to the glory of God the Father.*

I discovered this wonderful scripture as a kid, and I got an understanding that nothing can harm me when I am under the shield of the name of Jesus. Because the Bible says, no creature can keep his head up when the name of Jesus is mentioned as though the name crunches the bones in their knees to bow to the King of Kings.

Acts 3:3-11 talked about when Jesus Christ had ascended to heaven. Peter and John began to move around the city, healing the sick through the name of Jesus. There they met a man who was sick asking them for money, but see what they did. *"Who seeing Peter and John about to go into the temple asked an alms. And Peter, fastening his eyes upon him with John, said, Look at us. And he gave heed unto them, expecting to receive something of them. Then Peter said, Silver and gold have I none; but such as I have give I thee: In the name of Jesus Christ of Nazareth rise up and walk.*

And he took him by the right hand, and lifted him up: and immediately his feet and ankle bones received strength. And he leaping up stood, and walked, and entered with them into the temple, walking, and leaping, and praising God. And all the people saw him walking and praising God: and they knew that it was he which sat for alms at the Beautiful gate of the temple: and they were filled with wonder and amazement at that which had happened unto him.

*And the lame man which was healed held Peter and
John, all the people ran together unto them in the porch
that is called Solomon's, greatly wondering.*

After Peter healed the lame man, the people became
surprised and began to crowd around Peter and John on
the porch where they were sitting, which belongs to
Solomon. If you read further in that chapter, Peter
asked, "Why are you so surprised? Is it this lame man's
healing that makes you surprised?"

He went ahead to say, "The God of Abraham, Isaac, and
Jacob, this God of ours, glorified His servant Jesus,
whom you delivered up and denied in the presence of
Pilate when he was determined to let Him go. But you
denied the holy and just One. You asked for a murderer
to be granted to you and killed the prince of life, whom
God raised from the dead, of which we are all
witnesses."

Peter went further to say, "It is still this man you all
wanted dead; it was through this man's name. Through
faith in His name, God has made this lame man strong
and healed. This is the man you all knew as lame, now,
he is healed in the midst of you all."

Peter also addressed the rulers when they asked him
what power he used to heal and how he made them
believers of Christ. Peter answered, and I loved that he

had answers to all the questions he was asked. "Let it be known to you all and to all the people of Israel that by the name of Jesus Christ of Nazareth, whom you crucified and whom God raised from the dead, by Him this man stands here before you, whole (healed body and soul)."

Everyone witnessed the man walking. God's divine healing cannot be denied. Acts 4:14; *And beholding the man which healed standing with them, they could say nothing against it.* Because this was too real to be denied. As Papa would say, only a fool doubts proof.

God's divine healing has all the proof you need to trust in Him. Healing belongs to every believer. As believers, there are things you already have the right to, such as salvation, the gift of the Holy Spirit, divine healing, finances, and spiritual victory. Healing is for everyone, as Exodus 15:26 tells us; *And said, if thou wilt diligently hearken to the voice of the LORD thy God, and wilt do that which is right in his sight, and wilt give ear to his commandments, and keep all his statues, I will put none of these diseases upon thee, which I have brought upon the Egyptians: for I am the LORD that healeth thee.*

The name of Jesus works for everything. It carries power. There's a mighty power in the name if you use your faith. Everything about Christ is based on faith. If you don't believe it, how do you want it to work for you? You need to believe. This is so interesting: if you don't have faith, the faith of others can get you what you need.

There was a sceptic who never believed in Jesus, even on the verge of losing his life. He doubted and rubbished the things of God. He was slowly dying but still doubted that God could heal him. A few of his friends tried to share about Jesus with him, but he never listened to them, although he didn't make it obvious because he didn't want to be rude. But he cursed and mocked them in his mind.

His wife believed that Jesus could heal her husband. She didn't know much about Jesus due to her family background but she trusted Him nonetheless that He would heal him. She always stayed up late to pray and read her Bible. Then she started attending church to learn more about Jesus. Her husband was against her going to church. They fought and she cried about it.

As the day went on, his condition worsened, and he didn't have the strength to stop her from going to church anymore. He was dying from so much pain; it was dreadful. She would start crying too each time she sees his condition getting out of control.

She determined to take him to church with her one day. She told him that it was time to get healed, that Jesus heals, and that she has seen people get healed in church. Therefore, she believed it was her husband's turn to get healed. She had faith, her hope came alive, and she became joyful.

The sceptic husband refused to go with her. He called her faith 'nonsense', and screamed that there is no Jesus and that people going to church are mentally insane and needed to go for medical checkups.

She cried to him in her soft voice, saying, "Marcus, Jesus is real, trust me. I have faith that He can and will heal you." Her eyes were teary, and her voice was broken. Marcus couldn't withstand her tears. He hates seeing her cry. He thought about what she had been going through since he couldn't do anything for himself anymore.

He thought about how she weeps secretly in her room while cooking in the kitchen and while she does the laundry. She wept because all the burden was on her, including feeding the family with her salary. She was broken, and he hated that. He hated that he couldn't do anything to help himself or support his wife.

So the way she cried touched his heart. He agreed to go with her, as a favour, he thought. She had faith, so she took him to Kathryn Kuhlman's Sunday service, and as soon as he stepped inside the church, she had her hands around him to support him as he walked inside.

Immediately he sat, the glory of the Lord came upon him. The power of the Holy Spirit began to heal every damaged part of his body, and he heard a bone crack on his back. He was being fixed by Jesus.

As soon as the Holy Spirit was done with him, he rose to his feet without any help from the ushers or his wife. With tears, he called out his wife's name. He was confused and happy at the same time.

His wife screamed, "Marcus, you are healed! Oh my God, Jesus did it, Marcus. Thank you, Jesus!" She cried with a shaky voice. Marcus was still trying to process what had just happened to him; he was shocked that he could now walk and even jump.

Unknowingly, he screamed, "Thank you, Jesus!" She pulled him into a tight hug and said, "Marcus, I told you Jesus was real. I told you Jesus could heal you. I have so much faith in Him." She cried in his arms.

Then finally he said, "Yes, your Jesus is real, Lilian", and she replied, "Our Jesus is real. Have faith in Him from now on." she whispered.

"I will continue to have faith in Jesus from now on. Thank you, Lilian." He smiled and held out her hands as they approached the pulpit to share their testimony. There was overflowing peace in his heart. Jesus will give you peace. John 14:27: *Peace I leave with you; my peace I give to you. Not as the world gives, do I give to you. Let not your hearts be troubled, nor let them get afraid.* Jesus gives you this indescribable peace and joy.

So, friends, it takes faith for divine healing to work. The faith of others can heal you, as well as yours. Therefore, when you call the name of Jesus in any situation, call it with faith. See in Acts 3:16; *And his name through faith in His name hath made this man strong, whom ye see and know: yea, the faith which is by him hath given him this perfect soundness in the presence of you all.*

Through faith in the name of Jesus Christ, Paul was able to heal a crippled man at Lystra. The cripple had been hearing about him healing the sick and those oppressed by the spirit of sickness. So when he saw Paul, he sensed that Paul has the faith to heal him, even though he doesn't have the faith to be healed. He believed that the faith of Paul would get him healed. Acts 14:8-10; *And there sat a certain man at Lystra, impotent in his feet, being a cripple from his mother's womb, who never had walked: the same heard Paul speak: who stedfastly beholding him, and perceiving that he had faith to be healed, said with a loud voice, Stand upright on thy feet. And he leaped and walked.*

The name of Jesus does signs and wonders. Acts 4:30; *By stretching forth thine hand to heal; and that signs and wonders may be done by the name of thy holy child Jesus.*

Read testimonies from people who discovered Jesus and the power in His name:

A MAN HEALED FROM EPILEPSY AFTER HE DISCOVERED ABOUT JESUS

I experienced epilepsy for roughly 18 years. I gave up after trying everything I knew. On Good Friday, 2011, someone taught me about Christ, and I was reborn. I had had seizures the previous day.

I accepted Jesus a few weeks after Good Friday, and I was healed instantly. I will continue to tell people about Jesus and how He healed me. I have been strong in the Lord ever since. God bless you.

- By Michael

HEALED FROM A HEART DISEASE

My mother had a minor block and around this time, her heart was at its weakest. One day, she couldn't take it anymore, so we rushed her to the hospital. The blockage got severe and she couldn't breathe. Standing or sitting was a difficult task for her.

At the hospital, I did not care who was watching; I just knelt and prayed, "Lord, please let your healing come upon her, and let this be just a gas or something. Please, no operation, no hospital admission, no ambulance situations."

I prayed to Jesus Christ, pleading for Him to intercede for us, and I prayed to the Holy Spirit, asking Him to pray for us. Believe it or not, the doctors saw the report and said the exact thing I prayed for. It was gas that caused the problem, and she was only treated with medicines.

Fear not, for I am with you; be not dismayed; for I am thy God: I will strengthen thee; yea, I will help thee; yea, I will uphold thee with the right hand of my righteousness.

But when you pray, believe that our gracious Lord is hearing your prayers, and He will grant them. There is nothing our God cannot do. If you are reading this today, pray!

Praise our heavenly Father.

- By Mandira

HEALED FROM KIDNEY FAILURE

I woke up not feeling well and checked into a hospital close to my house. It turned out I had kidney failure, and one round of dialysis cleared me up. But I contracted a virus that started to paralyze me, and rather than deal with it, they put me in a coma on Friday. By Monday morning, I was on life support, and my family were saying goodbye. A hospital downtown took me in, operated on, and saved my life. I knew nothing of this and went there several times after the surgery. I could only move my eyes, as the surgery had left me a quadriplegic.

I looked around the room, trying to figure out what was happening. Suddenly, a warm feeling came over me near my head. I had a conversation in my head, with Jesus Christ. He said I should have complete faith in Him and He would take care of me. I was a recently born-again Christian, and I did exactly that. I had a positive attitude, knowing I would be okay. Seven years later, I'm still in a nursing home, but I can use my legs, and arms, and lift my legs. My kidney got healed. My life is good because of Jesus!

- By John Rek

COMPLETELY HEALED

A few years back, I was bedridden for almost three to four years. Due to the sickness, I could neither work nor earn. My doctor advised me in the second week of June to undergo surgery on both knees to be mobile again. This was because the lubricating fluid in my knee has dried up and it will cost me about $4 million. The surgery was scheduled for July 19th. I had no money, my haemoglobin count was below 7, and I was very weak.

This was so much that the doctor said that they will only consider the surgery on one of my knees if my haemoglobin count is at least 11. My blood group is B-negative, so it was difficult getting donors to donate blood. With so many drawbacks, my trust was only in God.

I prayed, "God, it is you who heals, with or without surgery, so if it is your will that I have to undergo surgery to walk again, please help me with the money needed."

God heard my prayer, and miraculously, the money was raised; my friends supported me, people came to donate blood (approximately 10 units), and on July 9th, my haemoglobin count was 12.

I went under the knife on both knees at the same time with no side effects The chief doctor, who came to see me in the ward after a few hours, said that they normally shift the patients to the ICU after the surgery, even if they had undergone surgery on one knee. But I was so healthy that he shifted me directly to the ward, after surgery on both knees. I thanked God and the doctors for a successful surgery.

I believe that it was Jesus who did my surgery. Thank you, Jesus; I am perfectly fine today!

-By Margret Rose

How do you pray for healing in the name of Jesus? "Lord, please heal my broken heart. Fill me with peace and joy. I know healing can only come from you. The journey to healing and recovery is possible through your power alone. In Jesus' name. Amen."

Jesus is awesome. He says, Call unto me, and I will rescue you. 1 Thessalonians 5:23; *And the very God of peace sanctify you wholly; and I pray God your whole spirit and soul and body be preserved blameless unto the coming of our Lord Jesus Christ.*

2. Through Anointing Oil

Is any sick among you? Let him call for the elders of the church; and let them pray over him, anointing him with oil in the name of the Lord. James 5:14

God, the healer, has given us another method for defeating the adversary and his schemes. The scripture says, Is anyone sick among you? Let him call for the elders of the church and let them pray for him, using the anointing oil. The holy anointing oil can therefore be used in the name of Jesus to heal anyone who is sick. Every person has access to healing.

Holy anointing oil is one of God's tremendous weapons that He gave His children, to destroy every satanic oppression in their lives, just as fear is one of the devil's strongholds against God's children.

The holy anointing oil is so powerful that it serves all purposes, including raising the dead, healing the sick, and rescuing us from attack and oppression. The healing power of God is in the oil, and applying the oil on you will unleash the healing power of God upon your health. See where God anointed His Son; *How God anointed Jesus of Nazareth with the Holy Ghost and with power; who went about doing good and healing all that were oppressed of the devil; for God was with him.* Acts 10:38

The anointing oil may look simple, but it is a great weapon in which God's power resides, and anywhere the great healing power dwells has become God's temple. There's power in God's house. Jacob had a dream and saw that in the place where he slept, God was there. Then he used the stones he had laid his head on to build a pillar, and he called it the house of God.

Genesis 28:10-22;

And Jacob went out from Beersheba and went towards Haran. And he lighted upon a certain place and tarried there all night, because the sun had set; and he took the stones of that place and put them for his pillows, and he lay down in that place to sleep.

And he dreamed, and behold, a ladder set up on the earth, and the top of it reached to heaven; and behold, the angels of God were ascending and descending on it. And, behold, the LORD stood above it and said, I am the LORD God of Abraham, thy father, and the God of Isaac: the land whereon thou liest, to thee will I give it, and to thy seed; and thy seed shall be as the dust of the earth, and thou shalt spread abroad to the west, to the east, to the north, and to the south; and in thee and in thy seed shall all the families of the earth be blessed.

And behold, I am with thee, and will keep thee in all places whither thou goest, and will bring thee again into this land; for I will not leave thee until I have done that which I have spoken to thee of. And Jacob awaked out of his sleep, and he said, Surely the LORD is in this place, and I knew it not. And he was afraid and said, How dreadful is this place! This is none other than the house of God, and this is the gate of heaven.

And Jacob rose up early in the morning and took the stone that he had put for his pillows and set it up for a pillar, and poured oil upon the top of it. And he called the name of that place Bethel, but the name of that city was called Luz at the first.

And Jacob vowed a vow, saying, "If God will be with me, and will keep me in this way that I go, and will give me bread to eat and clothing to put on, so that I come again to my father's house in peace, then shall the LORD be my God; and this stone, which I have set for a pillar, shall be God's house; and of all that thou shalt give me, I will surely give the tenth to thee."

The holy anointing oil is God's house, where children get protected from any evil. While it might seem too easy, God has preordained it for our healing and deliverance.

Anything the great physician resides in is not simple at all. It is powerful and we should be committed to it as it is what God has provided for our protection. Mark 6:12-13; *And they went out and preached that men should repent. And they cast out many devils, and anointed with oil many that were sick, and healed them.*

God is in the oil, and whoever gets anointed with the oil is activating God's power in it upon his or her life. Jesus Christ was anointed by God, and he went about doing mighty things; healing the sick and those who were oppressed by the devil, and God was with Him. The anointing oil on Him began to activate the power of God that resides in the oil upon His life. (Acts 10:38)

Whoever gets anointed with the holy oil of God becomes untouchable. No sickness, oppression, or affliction of the devil or man can affect him. Psalm 105:13-15: *When they went from one nation to another, from one kingdom to another people, he suffered no man to do them wrong; yea, he reproved kings for their sake, saying, Touch not mine anointed, and do my prophets no harm.*

Anointing yourself is giving God control over your life and the situation. Also, in 1 Chronicles 16:19-22; *When ye were but few, even a few, and strangers in it. And when they went from nation to nation and from one kingdom to another people, he suffered no man to do them wrong; yea, he reproved kings for their sakes, saying, Touch not mine anointed, and do my prophets no harm.*

It is like a security guard guarding a house. When you are anointed, you are being guarded by God. No sickness can torment you, and in the name of Jesus, using the anointing, you will get healed. Mark 6:13: *And they cast out many devils and anointed with oil many who were sick, and they healed them.*

See what 1 John 2:27 says; *But the anointing which ye have received from him abideth in you, and ye need not that any man teach you; but as the same anointing teacheth you of all things and is truth and is no lie, and even as it hath taught you, ye shall abide in him.*

As I said earlier, using the anointing oil is activating the power of God in it in your life. He abides in you as you have applied it, and you in Him. The anointing oil is like a seal, protecting you from sickness and the oppression of the devil. Do you remember when I called it the house of God? Can you imagine being under the shield of God's house? Nothing can harm you!

In the church I attend, a woman and her children's testimony were shared. She had a child of about 10 years old and another who was about 2 years old. On their way home from church, they set out in search of a new apartment; however, someone pointed them in the direction of a building that had an empty flat. They travelled there. She met some strange-looking men when she arrived, but she wasn't terrified because her God says fear not. When she asked them if there had been a vacancy, they responded with a resounding "yes."

She was asked to follow them while they survey the residence. The two men entered the vacant flat first, followed by her and the children. The door slammed behind them as soon as she walked in, startling her. When she realized that the door was closed, she was shocked. Why would they shut the door while merely surveying the apartment? That was terrifying.

She was unaware they were ritualists until they started reciting incantations. Normally, you would be scared, knowing you and the kids might not come out of that place alive. But she didn't fret. Instead, she laughed and said, "I pity you people. Do you know the God I serve?" She commanded them to open the door immediately if they value their lives.

The men scorned and mocked her, as though what she was saying was trash until her son screamed, "Holy Ghost fire!" and poured anointing oil on them and on the floor. Immediately, the place caught fire. They began to beg, scared of being burned to death, and after all, the door was locked.

The woman didn't fret still. She brought out her mantle from her bag, wiped it on the door and it opened! To God be all the glory, they got out of their trap successfully, and none of them was hurt.

This is it, friends. The anointing oil has the power of God in it. When you are anointed, you are protected everywhere you go. When I was young, I was taught how to pray after using the anointing oil, and whenever

I want to step out, I would use it. I apply the anointing and say the prayers; "I bear the mark of exemption in the name of Jesus."

Once I do that, I have full confidence that nothing can harm me, and it works!

One day, before I left home for school, I anointed myself with oil. I did that always then, and I still do. On my way to school, a car was about to drive out by my side but I didn't see it coming, and neither did the driver.

I was so close to it. I didn't even know someone was inside the car. But immediately the car drove near me at a high speed, something pushed me forward. It felt like an invisible force. I was surprised at what was happening until I saw the car move past me speedily. If that force had not pushed me forward, I would have been crushed by the car.

I'll never forget what happened that day. I began to cry and thank Jesus. I knew it was Jesus who saved me. I knew He was the invisible force that pushed me forward. When you are anointed, you become the apple of God's eye.

Nothing can harm an anointed one. He is capable of doing anything to protect His anointed one. Do you know how some unbelievers use charm as their power? In the same way, this holy anointing oil is like a power you have over those sicknesses and afflictions of the devil. Psalm 23:1-6; *The LORD is my shepherd; I shall not want. He maketh me to lie down in green pastures: he leadeth me beside the still waters. He restoreth my soul: He leadeth me in the paths of righteousness for his name's sake. Yea, though I walk through the valley of the shadow of death, I will fear no evil: for thou art with me; Thy rod and thy staff they comfort me.*

Thou preparest a table before me in the presence of mine enemies: thou anointed my head with oil; my cup runneth over. Surely goodness and mercy shall follow me all the days of my life: And I will dwell in the house of the LORD forever. This was David's prayer after he was anointed. He knew nothing could harm him because God was with him.

The Spirit of God comes upon you and is with you when you become anointed. When the Spirit of God is upon you, He manifests His power in your life. See where God asked Samuel to anoint His servant David, and the Spirit of God came upon him. 1 Samuel 16:11-14; *And Samuel said unto Jesse, Are here all thy children? And he said, There remaineth yet the youngest, and, behold, he keepeth the sheep. And Samuel said unto Jesse, send and fetch him: for we will not sit down till he come hither.*

And he sent, and brought him in. Now he was ruddy, and withal of a beautiful countenance, and goodly to look to. And the LORD said, Arise, anoint him: for this is he. Then Samuel took the horn of oil, and anointed him in the midst of his brethren: and the Spirit of the LORD came upon David from that day forward. So Samuel rose up, and went to Ramah.

As soon as he was anointed, the Holy Spirit began to manifest in David's life. He could do the supernatural - something beyond human capacity - and he knew it was the Holy Spirit at work in him.

When you are anointed, you begin to do the supernatural. No sickness can operate in the supernatural realm; therefore, sickness is defeated.

David began to do great things because the Holy Spirit was with him as the anointed one of God. There was a point he cried to God, pleading for Him not to take the Holy Spirit from him. Whenever he did something wrong, he would cry that God could take anything else from him. He said, "Take not the Holy Spirit from me." Psalm 51:11.

David knew how important the Holy Spirit was to him. The power of the Holy Spirit makes you extraordinary. This is the victory you have with the anointing oil.

The Oil Activates Your Faith for Healing

In heaven, there is no sickness, no disease, and no lack. The way it is in heaven, God wants the same for us on earth. He wants us to be healthy like supernatural beings and prosper in all things. 3 John 1:2; *Beloved, I wish above all things that thou mayest prosper and be in health, even as thy soul prospereth.*

In Psalm 105:14-15; *He suffered no man to do them wrong: Yea, he reproved kings for their sakes; saying, Touch not mine anointed, and do my prophets no harm.* This implies that no sickness, virus, or disease can harm or affect us. God protects us from what we cannot see, like the COVID-19 virus and invisible battles. We don't feel it because God fights for us.

One day, I had an encounter with God. We were discussing, and He asked, "Do you think people have not been trying to attack you?" But I've not felt anything; I sleep well, eat well, wake up healthy and feel good. But I had no idea I was being attacked.

Then He said, "Yes, they've been trying a lot of attacks on you, but I don't let them touch you!"

I gasped in amazement, slapping my hands across my mouth in shock. He told me I would have died, but He is the one who saves me from the invisible attacks I couldn't see. I began to cry and thank Him. God is worthy; He loves me, and I don't deserve this love, but

He loves me. He says nothing can separate us from His love, not even our sinful nature. He loves us!

Thus, the anointing oil stirs up our faith. There was a woman who was protected from the COVID-19 virus despite being in contact with someone who was infected. She had faith that nothing could harm her because she was anointed. It means she was exempted from the COVID-19 virus; therefore, the anointing oil made her immune to the virus.

A testimony was shared in church about anointing oil applied with faith. A brother had a kidney problem. He heard about the holy anointing oil and decided to use it, believing that God could heal him through the anointing oil. He drank a little, and the power of God began to work in him. He experienced a change in how he felt, as though something was going on inside him.

He believed God was working on him, so the next day, he went for another test. The result showed that his kidney has become brand new. Someone who had a kidney problem, through the anointing oil, got a new kidney.

It can only be God! The anointing oil burned up the chaff (disease) with an unquenchable fire. Matthew 3:12: *whose fan is in his hand, and he will throughly purge his floor and gather his wheat into the garner; but he will burn up the chaff with unquenchable fire.*

God can even heal your pet! How much more you? A pastor at school gave a testimony about his pet. It had an injury in one part of his left leg. The dog couldn't walk properly because of the wound. He knew about healing with the anointing oil and began to anoint his dog every day, without giving it any medication. He was never worried about the pet because he knew it was something God could do through the anointing oil. He forgot the dog was injured one day until it began to walk, looking very healthy. He then remembered that his pet was once hurt, so he went to check on the left leg. He saw that the leg was completely healed. There were no longer any bleeding or injuries. It all disappeared.

God can do great things through anointing oil. Unbelievable things; yes, because He is God!

When you put the oil on yourself, you come under God's shield, and nothing can harm you. He protects you from all plagues and evil.

Here is a shocking story I heard in a Sunday service. A man shared how he was able to defeat the devil over his granddaughter's life. On the day of the naming ceremony, the baby suddenly became cold and was no longer breathing. Her mother was not around; she went to dress her hair for the ceremony.

He carried her and saw that she was dead. He didn't believe it, so he called his wife to see what was happening. She shook the baby but there was no response, and neither did she cry. She confirmed the baby was dead. Immediately the old man screamed, "It is a lie! She cannot die. Give me the baby." He took the baby and carried her to her room.

He laid her on the bed, brought out his bottle of anointing oil, and said, "There's power in the oil, baby, you cannot die." He said this as he applied the oil to her forehead. Then he went to get his mantle.

He began to wipe the mantle on the baby, saying, "You spirit of death, leave her in the name of Jesus!" He repeated this three times. He switched to the next prayer point while still using the anointing oil and the mantle. He said, "Baby, come back to life! In the name of Jesus, come back!" He said this twice.

The baby jerked back to life on the third count! She shook her hands and opened her eyes. Glory to God!

The devil attempted to take the baby's life again, and he used the same method to defeat him. Today, the baby is alive and healthy.

God is always ready to protect and deliver His anointed ones from the hands of the devil.

3. Taking God's Word as Medicine

My son, attend to my words; incline thine ear unto my sayings. Let them not depart from thine eyes; keep them in the midst of thine heart. For they are life unto those that find them, and health to all their flesh. Proverbs 4:20-22.

God's word is the perfect solution for every sickness. In every situation, there is a word of God to resolve it. Friends, no solution can't be found in God's word. If you are sick, you will find the solution in His word. If you have anxiety, God's word has the solution for it. If you are confused, God's word is available to settle your awkward thoughts, and if you are desperate for money, God's word is available to heal you from those toxic thoughts.

Some days back, I came across this scripture; Ecclesiastes 6:7–12. I got answers to questions that has been running through my mind. This scripture gave me the answers. One of the questions was; why would people go to work every day, and work extremely hard just to earn money? The money would finish in a blink of an eye, then you have to work again to earn money which will finish. This cycle feels like a setback. The author of 'Rich Dad and Poor Dad' called it the rat race. I ask, why do we have to continue the race when it proves that we can get nothing out of it?

The second question was; no matter how much people make, they never get satisfied. Why? This scripture will give you the answers the same way it gave me answers.

Ecclesiastes 6:7-12; *All the labour of man is for his mouth, and yet the appetite is not filled. For what hath the wise more than the fool? What hath the poor, that knoweth to walk before the living? Better is the sight of the eyes than the wandering of the desire: this is also vanity and vexation of spirit.*

That which hath been is named already, and it is known that it is man: neither may he contend with him that is mightier than he. Seeing there be many things that increase vanity, what is man the better? For who knoweth what is good for man in this life, all the day of his vain life which he spendeth as a shadow? For who can tell a man what shall be after him under the sun?

The solution was in God's word. Humans work for money constantly and are never pleased with what they get, and it always disappears into thin air. The Bible declares that all of these endeavours are vain. A man won't benefit from it in any way. Being desperate for money is a result of the vexation of the spirit. Therefore, friends, God's word contains the answer to every problem.

The word of God is a cure-for-all. It is a medication that can treat both the body and the soul. The only thing that can heal the soul is the word of God; no drug can do that. I learnt that no medicine can heal completely; doctors just prescribe drugs to maintain health, lessen pain, and perhaps treat; only God has the power to heal permanently.

A medical professional once said, "Once a patient, always a patient." I asked her why she said so. Her response was, "Darling, no one should ever become ill; if they do, they will always be patients because they'll have to visit their doctors for therapy and checkups regularly. God is everything to us, sweetie. We all depend on Him." Only God can cure. You can only be freed from being a patient by God.

The world's top doctors openly acknowledged that the advances made in medical research have not been sufficient to eliminate or fight sicknesses and diseases. Doctors can only do what they know because their knowledge is limited. They will inevitably come across things for which they have no cure. God's knowledge is unlimited, and He has given us that knowledge in His word.

Unlike doctors, there are no mistakes or wrong prescriptions in God's word. In the worst scenarios, their treatments have led to the deaths of patients. Doctors are humans too, and humans are prone to making mistakes. It is inevitable. So, will you rather trust God for your healing or trust in humans whose knowledge is limited? It is your choice to make.

We need to develop the ability to turn to God's words and employ them as a remedy. God will always be your healer.

Whatever sickness or disease you have, God's word has the power to heal you completely. God's word has the power to heal every ailment, and what's even more astonishing is that it costs you nothing. There's no overdose, and neither will it hurt. You will rather be more edified and alive as a result.

Ephesian 4:29; *Let no corrupt communication proceed out of your mouth, but that which is good to the use of edifying, that it may minister grace unto the hearers.*

God's word is a medicine, and taking too much of it will strengthen your body and soul, unlike medications which could worsen your health. The Bible says in Acts 20:32; *And now, brethren, I commend you to God, and to the word of His grace, which is able to build you up, and to give you the inheritance among all them which are sanctified.*

When we are sick, we can take doses of this priceless medicine, just like we would a prescription from a doctor. I have done this often and I know some of my friends and other believers who have done the same. Taking the word of God as medicine has cured migraine headaches, kidney infections, paralysis from strokes, broken bones, cancer, tuberculosis, mental deficiencies, and many other sicknesses of the body and soul. I read a testimony where a man's wound was healed by the word of God.

"Several years ago, when we moved into a new house, I was removing some trash from a large black plastic bag, and as I grabbed the bag to put it on the trailer, a razor blade in the trash slid through the third finger of my left hand, deep into the bone. Blood gushed everywhere, and in the natural setting, it would have required a lot of stitches. I wrapped a handkerchief around it and began to remind God about His words, and I began to meditate and speak the words to the wound as if I were talking to a doll.

The Holy Spirit then reminded me about the word of God in Ezekiel 16:6: *'And when I passed by thee and saw thee polluted in thine own blood, I said unto thee when thou wast in thy blood, Live; yea, I said unto thee when thou wast in thy blood, Live!'*

This word of God became a medicine for my flesh. I spoke it out and believed it could be a reality for me right away. I released the power of the word by faith, and I commanded the blood flow to slow down, and within a couple of hours, there was only a white mark where there should have been several stitches."

The way you visit a doctor to have him prescribe you medicine is the same way you should approach God's word for healing. You have to pick up the word of God and digest it the same way you do drugs. Take God's word as your medicine!

Search for scriptures that relate to your illness or those that pertain to your spirit. Read them and medicate your body with them. They were written for you. You should go there repeatedly, the same way you take drugs repeatedly. I know believers who read their scripture every fifteen minutes for several days.

In one of his testimonies, Derek Prince described a challenge that even a prolonged hospital stay could not resolve or cure. His doctor advised him to avoid intense heat and moisture as those two conditions would severely worsen his condition, and that they had to discharge him without curing him. Regrettably, those two circumstances were all he had to work with while stationed at his military job. Nevertheless, he had developed the belief that God's word can be used as medication by the time he was diagnosed.

He made time after each meal every day for several months to read the word of God as if he were taking a doctor's prescription. Psalm 107:20: *He sent his word, and healed them and delivered them from their destructions.* Some months later, Derick became healed without medication, and he could finally go back to his job.

When you fill your thoughts with the word of God, you become healed mentally, emotionally, physically, and spiritually. Yes, God can also heal emotionally. If you are suffering from toxic emotions, God can heal you. God can heal you from any kind of mental disorder as well. God can heal bipolar disorder!

Sometimes, emotional pain can be too painful to move on from and can hurt more than physical injuries. It is a kind of wound that is invisible to the physical eyes, and it hurts as though your heart has been pierced with a knife. I was once vandalized emotionally, and it hurt in my chest like a burning flame. It was dreadful and inconvenient. I was the only one who could feel the pain as if I had been physically hurt within. And no matter how much I explained it to my loved ones, they couldn't relate, and that hurts more.

Since no one could understand me and I was afraid it could be something more complicated, I turned to God. I prayed to God to heal me of the pain in my heart. It was due to hurtful words and rejection from peers.

Thank God that I knew God was my healer; I cried to Him whenever it starts to ache and whenever the pain becomes unbearable as if they were real wounds. I kept on telling God to heal me because I could no longer take it, and one day, I found out that the pain was gone. I no longer feel it!

Sometimes, the absence of parental love, the pain of rejection, betrayal, the emotional horror of rape, or the unexplainable sorrow of losing a child, spouse, or anyone you deeply love can seem incurable, but it is never incurable to God. He is never comfortable seeing His children in that kind of grief and sorrow.

I read a story in one of Kathryn's books. It happened on Christmas day. Joe and Dora had two boys; one was about ten years old, and the other was about eight years old. The morning was cold and snowy, and her husband had to go to work that morning. He would be back as early as possible to spend the remaining part of the day with his family. Joe was about to step out of the house when Mike, his eight-year-old son, called out for him.

"Daddy! Please don't go yet. I have a surprise for you. I want you to see it before you go." There was excitement in his voice. Joe had to let go of the doorknob, turning back to see Mike dragging down some boxes mounted above his face from the stairs. It was bigger than him, so Joe stopped him. "Mike, you don't have to bring it down here. Daddy will go up to meet you if you can't come to meet him." Joe shared a brilliant smile with Dora and a warm kiss on her forehead before he went upstairs to meet Mike.

Joe saw the surprise and ran back to the door. He had to leave if he wanted to spend more time with them later. Steve, their ten-year-old, screamed, "Daddy, we will be waiting for you!" He smiled, kissing them again before heading out.

Because it was Christmas, Dora had a lot to do, especially in the kitchen. She was trying to chop the vegetables when the boys ran to her, wanting to go out to play with other kids. Since Dora needed time to take care of the things she needed to get done, she permitted the kids to go out to play.

It was cold, so she knew they would be back soon. She chuckled because she knew they would run back in a minute or two. She kept busy with the vegetables until she heard a knock at the door. She thought it was the kids, so she ran to let them in. But she was surprised to see her neighbour on the porch; she wasn't only standing there, she was sobbing as well, which got Dora a little confused.

"What's wrong, Christina?" she asked, taking off the glove from her hands. "Something bad has happened, Dora." Her words escaped with a puff of steam from her lips, and they were trembling, including her fingers.

Dora asked what was wrong, and then she said, "Two boys fell into the pond." She exhaled. "I think they are your boys."

Dora's heart jumped to her throat immediately. Her eyes became red and teary. She didn't believe it; she thought Christina was mistaken because her boys just came outside to play. "I think you are mistaken, Christina. My boys are just by the corner playing," she said in a cracking voice.

"You might want to come with me; I will show you," Christina said. Dora ran inside to get something thick; she was restless. When she followed Christina, people were already crowding the pond, and the FBI had arrived as well, so no one could go close to the pond. It was 38 feet deep.

She screamed as though she were going crazy, "No! They are my babies! Please, my babies, I need to go in there! I don't care, I just need to go into the pond with my babies, please!" She cried, screaming in frustration because she could see her boys iced over in the pond. They must have been frozen to death.

It was painful. Her husband was informed, and he ran back home as soon as possible, to see his boys already dead. He was disabled for a year afterwards. It was terrible to move on from that kind of loss. They hadn't known about Jesus then, especially Joe, who hated things about Christ. He never believed in Jesus, until one day, a man preached to him and asked if he had encountered Jesus or if he had known Jesus.

His answer was negative. Joe thought that it was about time he knew who this Jesus was. Who is this Jesus that people have been talking about? Joe felt empty and sad over the loss of his boys. They were so innocent. They were waiting for him to come back home. They had surprises for their dad. Joe couldn't forget Steve's last words. "Daddy, we will be waiting for you!"

Joe was devastated for a year. He was always crying. He missed his boys; he frequently parked by the roadside to cry. It was dreadful; everywhere was filled with memories of his boys. He was helping a woman get some work done one sunny day, and he saw stockings that were about the size of Mike's. Then he began to cry again. He was broken. He was so broken that he didn't know where to start.

In that state, he thrived on knowing about Jesus. Who was this Jesus? He heard that Jesus gives unusual peace and heals the heart from sorrow. He attended a church service for the first time in his life, along with his wife. Jesus began to repair him; he began to feel alive again and have hope. He heard his kids were in heaven, and if he wanted to meet them again, the only way was through Jesus.

Joe and Dora became well again. They began to tell people about Jesus and how He had healed them from their trauma. Their faces were so radiant and full of joy, that their neighbour began to follow them to church. They became counsellors for parents who had also lost their kids. They became alive in hope because of Jesus. Jesus healed their grief!

Jesus heals wounds that cannot be cured through surgery, medication, or advice; only God can heal those kinds of wounds. See Psalm 147:3; *He healeth the broken in hearts and binds up their wounds.* And in Hebrew 4:15-16; *For we have not an high priest which cannot be touched with the feeling of our infirmities; but was in all points tempted as we are, yet without sin. Let us therefore come boldly unto the throne of grace, that we may obtain mercy, and find grace to help in time of need.*

The high priest is Jesus.

Jesus was once tempted on earth, so He knows exactly how it feels to be human in every aspect. This is why He is ready to comfort those with incurable wounds. He has endured all that we will ever endure as regards temptations, sorrow, pains, and more. He has overcome it, and He can take those pains away from us. Isaiah 53:4-5; *Surely he hath borne our griefs and carried our sorrows; yet we did esteem him stricken, smitten of God, and afflicted. But he was wounded for our transgressions; he was bruised for our iniquities; the chastisement of our peace was upon him, and with his stripes we are healed.* So friends, have you surrendered your emotional baggage to the one who can heal it?

Dr Lillian Yeomans is a medical doctor who experienced divine healing and walked away from her medical practice to minister healing through God's word. She had a patient in the last stage of tuberculosis. She began to read her verses from Deuteronomy 28 for several days, which referred to her specific condition.

The patient was almost dead and had no faith, to begin with, but she gradually became strong enough to read for herself, and as she did, the word stirred up faith in her heart. She jumped from her bed completely healed by the word of God.

A lady shared a testimony of how she used God's word as medicine to save her loved one. "One of those times, a concerned relative was experiencing some very alarming physical problems. One day, he suddenly began having severe chest pain and feeling extremely weak and sleepy. By the next day, he could hardly stay awake at all, and when he was awake, his speech was sluggish and slurred. He had a personal physician whom he saw periodically, but in this case, he decided to receive his healing from the Lord rather than go through all the medical channels. I prayed and called other believers to agree with me in prayers.

The symptoms persisted, and my cousin lay in bed almost constantly asleep. He was unable to stay up and alert for any lengthy periods. As I sat beside his bed on the worst day, praying and speaking the word, the Lord directed me to His word from Psalm 118:16–17. I grasped it like a life preserver, which it was. I knew the promise was for this man as much as it is for anyone because the Word says, 'Every promise is already answered 'yes' in Jesus.' (see 2 Cor. 1:20). So I put his name in the scripture and began to speak it to him: 'The right hand of the Lord does valiantly. Richard shall not die, but live and tell of the works of the Lord.'

I realized that this one verse had everything he needed at the time. It covered his need for life to drive out death, which was at work, and his need for restoration of his speaking faculties. I spoke that word to him consistently throughout the day, whether he was awake or asleep. I sat beside the bed for a long period, saying it over and over again. By the next day, he showed improvement. I continue to speak God's word, and he continued to improve, reading and speaking the Word for himself as well. By the following week, he was back to normal, and for the rest of his long life, he never had a recurrence of that problem, nor could his doctor find any cause or need for treatment concerning it later on. God's word healed him completely."

Your healing is tied to God and His word. God heals, and so do His words. God and His words are one. As God is powerful and mighty, His words are also powerful and mighty. John 1:1 says, *In the beginning was the Word, and the Word was with God, and the Word was God.*

The Word can heal us because we were created from it. God spoke the Word, and man came forth, and man began to have life, which was also from the Word. If we are sick, the Word can make us whole because it has its particles in us. It is as though the Word is an atom and we are the particles in it.

In chemistry, when an atom gets excited (noble), it affects everything in it, which are the particles (proton, electron, and neutron). The Word is life; now if it is proclaimed into our lives, we become like the Word, we have life. As an atom is excited and the particles gain rank, we gain life! We are part of the Word, and the Word is part of us!

Genesis 1:26-27: *And God said, Let us make man in our image, after our likeness; and let them have dominion over the fish of the sea, and over the fowl of the air, and over the cattle, and over all the earth, and over every creeping thing that creepeth upon the earth. So God created man in his own image; in the image of God, he created him; male and female, he created them.*

God spoke the word to the dust and man was made; He breathed into his nostrils to have life. Now that Word was what brought man forth, it means man is a product of the Word. Therefore, it can also heal man when he is sick. It is like flesh covering damaged flesh to make it healthy again. See in John 1:14: *And the Word was made flesh, and dwelt among us; (and we beheld his glory, the glory as of the only begotten of the Father), full of grace and truth.*

The Word and man are like bones connected to become one. This is why the Word can heal men. God's words heal.

The wife of a minister was diagnosed with 'incurable' cancer, and she was given a few months to live. She decided it was not her time to die and looked to God's word for life. She began meditating on the word of God regarding her healing and she fed on the scriptures every day and night. Her symptoms did not get better immediately, but she kept taking God's word as medicine, saying it to God and herself throughout the day. She kept renewing her mind with the word and rejecting doubt until she could 'see' herself getting well according to the promises of God. Contrary to the doctor's prognosis, she is alive today, after many years, totally healed, and still serving Jesus. God's word is medicine and life to our flesh.

Meditation on the Word

It is necessary to meditate on His word for success (complete healing). The word must be practical to add value or make itself manifest in our lives. In the event of an emergency, we must be rooted in God's word. That is why Jude 1:20–21 says, *But you, beloved, building yourselves up on your most holy faith, praying in the Holy Ghost, keep yourselves in the love of God, looking for the mercy of the Lord Jesus Christ unto eternal life.*

This scripture helps us understand that being rooted in the Word will benefit us in times of trials and tribulations (sickness). There was a man who was attacked by a sudden, severe headache. He began to recite the word of God, saying, "In the name of Jesus, by His stripes, I am healed." He kept reciting those words until he was healed of the severe headache. Now, because these words have been rooted in him, he was able to fight the headache, which is the tribulation he overcame. The word has to be rooted in you through meditation. See what Psalm 1:2; *But his (the man's) delight is in the law of the Lord, and in His law does he meditates day and night.*

Meditation on the Word makes it become part of us; even in our dreams, we can recite the Word that we instil in ourselves. I was sleeping one night and had a dream of being attacked by the devil. It felt like I was being pressed. Then I suddenly quoted a verse with authority, Luke 10:19. It says, *'Behold, I give unto you power to tread on serpents and scorpions and over all the power of the enemy; and nothing shall by any means hurt you.* I said this to the devil and defeated him in my dream because I knew I had been given power over the devil according to Luke 10:19. Because this word has been instilled in me and it had become part of me, I was able to defeat the devil with it in my dream.

Joshua 1:8 says, *"This book of the law shall not depart from your mouth, but you shall meditate on it day and night, so that you may be careful to do according to all that is written in it; for then you will make your way prosperous, and you shall have success."*

Meditating on the word of God also means making its works manifest in our lives. If you are sick, the more you study the word, meditate and say it out, the more it works its way into your system, giving you life. A brother who was sick learned about meditating on God's word, so he dived into this free opportunity for healing. He began to meditate on Psalm 23:1, saying it to himself over and over again: "The Lord is my shepherd; I shall not want."

He recited that verse about 50 times as he pondered on Jesus being a good shepherd and how kind He is to provide, lead, and heal him. Afterwards, every breath seems to release deep waves of healing throughout his being. The pain in his back disappeared, and by the time he got home, it was gone!

4. Laying of Hands

Neglect not the gift that is in thee, which was given thee by prophecy, with the laying on of the hands of the presbytery. 1 Timothy 4:14.

The laying on of hands is one of the secrets to accessing healing from God. We are not aware of this because we see our hands as ordinary, for holding, doing things, and eating, but we never see them as something that carries God's power.

We view our hands so ordinarily, whereas God sees them as having great potential for blessing, miracles, and healing. Our hands can do wonders because God has appointed them as keys to heal the sick and do anything that is God's will.

In the Bible, Jesus used laying-on of hands often. He laid His hands on the sick, and they became healed. The blind began to see as well. See in Mark 8:22–25: *And he came to Bethsaida; and they brought a blind man to him and besought him to touch him. And He took the blind man by the hand and led him out of the town; and when he had spit on his eyes and put his hands upon him, he asked him if he saw ought.*

And he looked up and said, I see men as trees, walking. After that, he put his hands again upon his eyes and made him look up; and he was restored and saw every man clearly.

After Jesus left, the disciples took over because it was a key that Jesus had taught them to use.

They began to lay hands on the sick. This method is still applicable in the church today; the laying on of hands is of this end time. 2 Timothy 1:6: *Wherefore I put thee in remembrance that thou stir up the gift of God, which is in thee, by the putting on of my hands.*

Jesus used the laying on of hands to perform some of his healing. Luke 4:38–39: *And he arose out of the synagogue and entered Simon's house. And Simon's wife's mother was taken with a great fever, and they besought him for her. And he stood over her and rebuked the fever, and it left her; and immediately she arose and ministered unto them.*

The laying on of hands is for everyone as long as you are a believer. The scripture doesn't say the anointed or the evangelist or the healing ministers alone; it says 'you'. Hebrew 6:2: *Of the doctrine of baptisms, and of the laying on of hands, and of the resurrection of the dead, and of eternal judgment.*

The scripture says you and I must be effective in the laying on of hands. He has put everything in our hands. God has ordained us in His word. John 3:35 says, *The Father loveth the son, and hath given all things into his hand.*

We are to use our hands to save the lost, heal the sick, deliver the oppressed, and finance the end-time harvest. A few days ago, I felt dizzy and weak. It started from my head, so I laid my hands on it and rebuked the sickness. Immediately, I was better. Then I continued with my work. There are powers in our hands; you all need to know this secret. Proverbs 3:27: *Withhold not good from them to whom it is due, when it is in the power of thine hand to do it.*

In Luke 13:11–13, Jesus healed a woman who had been sick for eighteen years by laying His hands on her. *"And, behold, there was a woman who had a spirit of infirmity for eighteen years and was bowed together and could in no wise lift herself up. And when Jesus saw her, he called her to him and said unto her, Woman, you are loosed from thine infirmity. And he laid his hands on her, and immediately she was made straight and glorified God."*

Hence, friends, you can be healed through the laying on of hands!

CHAPTER EIGHT

DON'T LIMIT GOD AND MISS YOUR HEALING

And when Jesus came into the ruler's house, and saw the minstrels and the people making a noise, He said unto them, give place: for the maid is not dead, but sleepeth. And they laughed him to scorn. But when the people were put forth, he went in, and took her by the hand and the maid arose. And the fame hereof went abroad into all that land. Matthew 9:23-26

The people scorned him because they thought that no matter what Jesus did, it wouldn't help as she was already dead. God disdains such attitude or mindset.

This kind of attitude can cause you to miss your healing. It is called "doubting God", which equals "lack of faith."

Ninety percent of this book is about faith. Faith is the ultimate force to move the hand of God. Jesus healed all who came to Him through faith. Apostle Peter healed individuals and multitudes through faith. Also, Paul had an exceptional account of ministering divine healing. Philip performed miracles with the same faith. Acts 6:5-7; *And the saying pleased the whole multitude: and they chose Stephen, a man full of faith and of the Holy Ghost, and Philip, and, Prochorus, and Nicanor, and Timon, and Parmenas, and Nicolas a proselyte of Antioch:*

Whom they set before the apostles: and when they had prayed, they laid their hands on them. And the word of God increased; and the number of disciples multiplied in Jerusalem greatly; and a great company of the priests were obedient to the faith.

God wants every individual to be able to perform miracles of healing without being an apostle because the faith the apostles used to heal is the same faith we also have. You do not need to be an apostle to heal; as a child of God, you are entitled to that same grace, the kind of grace that the apostles had in the Bible. Jesus said if you have faith as tiny as a mustard seed, you can move the mountain. See what Matthew 17:20 says; *And Jesus said unto them, because of your unbelief: for verily I say unto you, if ye have faith as a grain of mustard seed, ye shall say unto this mountain, remove hence to yonder place; and it shall remove; and nothing shall be impossible unto you.*

Do you know that when Jesus was still with the disciples, they also lacked faith? They couldn't heal a little child that was brought to them. See in Matthew 17:15-20; *Lord, have mercy on my son, for he is lunatick, and sore vexed: for ofttimes he falleth into the fire, and often into the water. And I brought him to thy disciples, and they could not cure him. Then Jesus answered and said, O faithless and perverse generation, how long shall I be with you? How long shall I suffer with you? Bring him hither to me.*

And Jesus rebuked the devil; and he departed out of him: and the child was cured from that very hour. Then came the disciples to Jesus apart, and said, why could not we cast him out? And Jesus said unto them, because of your unbelief: for verily I say unto you, if ye have faith as a grain of mustard seed, ye shall say unto this mountain, Remove hence to yonder place; and it shall remove; and nothing shall be impossible unto you.

As soon as Jesus Christ departed, they began to do the work of the Father much more than Jesus did. Yes, Jesus did say we would do mightier things than him. John 14:12; *Verily, verily, I say unto you, He that believeth on me, the works that I do shall he do also; and greater works than these shall he do; because I go unto my Father.*

Also, in Mark 9:17-25, there was someone with a dumb spirit and the disciples couldn't heal him because of lack of faith. *"And one of the multitudes answered and said, Master, I have brought unto thee my son, which hath a dumb spirit; And wheresoever he taketh him, he teareth him: and he foameth, and gnasheth with his teeth, and pineth away: and I spake to thy disciples that they should cast him out; and they could not.*

He answereth him, and saith, O faithless generation, how long shall I be with you? How long shall I suffer you? Bring him unto me. And they brought him unto Him: and when he saw him, straightway the spirit tare him; and he fell on the ground, and wallowed foaming. And he asked his father, How long is it ago since this came unto him? And he said, of a child.

And ofttimes it hath cast him into the fire, and into the waters, to destroy him: but if thou canst do any thing, have compassion on us, and help us. Jesus said unto him, if thou canst believe, all things are possible to him that believeth. And straightway the father of the child cried out, and said with tears, Lord, I believe; help thou mine unbelief. When Jesus saw that the people came running together, he rebuked the foul spirit, saying unto him, Thou dumb and deaf spirit, I charge thee no more into him, and enter no more into him."

Humans are limited, but not God. 1 Kings 8:27; *But will God indeed dwell on the earth? Behold, the heaven of heavens cannot contain thee; how much less this house that I builded?*

We have a mighty God who is unlimited, powerful, wonderful, and majestic. Nothing is difficult for Him to do. But somehow, in this generation, we limit God and question if He can do more than we ask or think. Some people would rather trust in gods that do not have ears to hear, mouths to speak, or eyes to see than trust in the living God. Some let doubt shorten the hands of God upon their lives.

It is this doubt that robs us of seeing the miracles He has done for us and the promises that He plans to fulfil in our lives. No matter what, believe God! Because God is able to do exceedingly great things. See Ephesians 3:20; *Now unto Him that is able to do exceedingly, abundantly above all that we ask or think, according to the power that worketh in us.*

Romans 4:18; *Who against hope believed in hope, that he might become the father of many nations, according to that which was spoken, So shall thy seed be.* This scripture shows that there was no hope for Abraham. He was old and Sarah had passed menopause, yet he didn't doubt or curse God one day. There was no reason to believe it was possible. It was a hopeless case, but something within him refused to doubt God.

Let's read further to verses 19-21; *And being not weak in faith, he considered not his own body now dead, when he was about an hundred years old, neither yet the deadness of Sara's womb: He staggered not at the promise of God through unbelief; but was strong in faith, giving glory to God. And being fully persuaded that, what he had promised, he was able also to perform.*

Friends, unbelief can limit the healing power of God in your life. He desires to heal you, but you can restrict Him by doubting and limiting His mighty power. You might think your sickness is too complicated, but according to His words, He heals all diseases. Psalm 103:2-3; *Bless the LORD, O my soul, and forget not all his benefits: Who forgiveth all thine iniquities; who healeth all thy diseases.*

He will heal all your diseases. Therefore, whatever the sickness is, do not limit God. Exodus 15:26; *And said, if thou wilt diligently hearken to the voice of the LORD thy God, and wilt do that which is right in his sight, and wilt give ear to his commandments, and keep all his statues, I will put none of these diseases upon thee, which I have brought upon the Egyptians: for I am the*

LORD that healeth thee. God is not the afflicter of sickness; He is the healer of sickness.

A sick lady once said to me: "Maybe God is not willing to heal me quickly, but rather, He's using this to teach me a lesson and as an example to bless others." No! God will never teach His children through sickness. And you are not Jesus Christ, so He should not use you as an example to bless others. He used Jesus Christ to bless and redeem you because He loves you.

God doesn't heal slowly to teach you a lesson. His words in Mark 1:41 were, "I am willing." God is willing to heal you anytime.

Mark 1:40-41; ***And there came a leper to him, beseeching him, and kneeling down to him, and saying unto him, if thou wilt, thou canst make me clean. And Jesus, moved with compassion, put forth his hand, and touched him, and saith unto him, I WILL; be thou clean.***

Don't limit God in the realm of healing. He desires to heal; He is willing to heal you.

God's power is unlimited, unfettered, and all-encompassing. A friend was sick and needed to see a doctor to know the cause of the illness. I told her she doesn't need to see a physician to become well, "because I believe if you speak to our Father about it, He will heal you."

She didn't buy the idea. She thought she needed to know what was wrong before she could ask God for healing. Her response was, "I know Ronny. I know God can heal me, but don't I need to know the cause of the sickness before God can know what to heal me of? You know, I have to be specific before God."

Logically, she was right; we need to be specific, but God doesn't need our human knowledge to heal us. That was her limiting God's power of healing. She thought that if she didn't know the cause and specifically ask God, then He wouldn't heal her. No! It is never so.

Do not limit the power of God, for He doesn't operate in the same realm as humans. Humans try to limit God in their reasoning. How can you let that happen when He is the creator of those brains?

Whatever is hurting you, whether you know the cause or not, never limit God. He is the God of all. He is the master of the universe. He is the omnipresent God. Do you think He does not know the cause of your sickness or the pain you are going through?

He knows everything! He knows your pains and sicknesses; you just need to tap into the flow of His healing power by faith, and not doubt.

A few days ago, someone dear to me complained of stomach ache. He explained that the pain was spreading to his heart. I felt great discomfort after his complaints. When he said he needed to run a test or get checked up to know the cause of the pain, I told him that he can be healed by the power of God no matter what the pain is. I appreciated that he didn't argue with me; his response was, "All right, amen."

That same day, as I was praying in the Holy Ghost, my left palm began to heat up. The Holy Spirit told me to rub my hot palm on his stomach. I did, and I said to him, "You are healed by the power of the Holy Spirit in Jesus' name. Amen!" I told him he was healed and he said he was going to observe it. I replied, "Sure! God has done His miracle on you."

This young man observed and confirmed he was healed of that pain, the pain he has been battling with for 14 years. It was a miracle and he shared his testimony with our prayer group.

"I have been battling with stomach pain since I was young. At first, it was minor, so I ignored it, but as time went on, the pain got intense. I had to select the kind of meals to eat and the kind of drugs to take; I eat as early as possible, in moderate quantities. There were so many conditions, I can't mention them all.

None of these improved the situation. So, I got fed up and gave up on drugs; they all failed. I became used to the pain and did its bidding daily. But all this ended yesterday evening when the Holy Spirit healed me of the sickness through Roanna.

Sir Goodnews shared the testimony yesterday, but I wasn't sure of my healing, that was why I didn't come out to share it then. So, I gave it a test today. I didn't eat or drink anything for the entire day and I felt no pain, which was unusual. It felt like I was filled without eating. I am completely healed by the Holy Spirit."

He didn't limit God, and he was healed miraculously.

Deal With Your Doubt

Abraham was one of the men who never doubted God in the Bible, no matter how impossible it seemed. He was told to leave his father's house with nothing. If it was someone in our generation, he would never obey because of doubts and fear. The question "What if?" arise from doubt.

Questions like; what if I don't get a place to stay? What if I starve to death because I had to leave my father's house? What if I never survive? These are the kind of questions that a man of our generation would have if he were in Abraham's shoes. But this man never doubted God! He said, "God instructed; I need to obey." Then he left his father's house.

I understand that some situations may seem impossible, but trust God. He is the King of Kings; He can do anything. Abraham never doubted God when he needed a child. He was a hundred years old, but his faith never wavered; neither did he consider himself too old or Sara, whose womb would have been dead. He didn't limit God's power. He let God do things His way. Romans 4:19-20; *And being not weak in faith, he considered not his own body now dead, when he was about a hundred years old, neither yet the deadness of Sara's womb. He staggered not at the promise of God through unbelief but was strong in faith, giving glory to God.* He trusted God without weakening his faith.

There is a connection between doubt and the weakening of our faith; a close relationship. Wavering leads to doubts, and doubt leads to unbelief, and unbelief creates an environment where faith will starve and die.

Fear and doubts are deserts where faith cannot survive. You need to kill and bury your doubts for your faith to stay alive.

See how the people of Israel doubted God and made God angry in Psalm 78:19–22; *yea, they spoke against God; they said, Can God furnish a table in the wilderness? Behold, he smote the rock, so that the waters gushed out and the streams overflowed; can he give bread also? Can he provide flesh for his people?*

Therefore, the LORD heard this and was wroth (angry), so a fire was kindled against Jacob, and anger also came up against Israel. Because they believed not in God and trusted not in his salvation.

We limit God's healing power when we start raising questions and doubts. We end up with unbelief, causing us to miss our healing because we don't trust God and His promises. This displeases God.

Donald Shaw once said, "How tragic that we humans, in our humanness, tend to fear and doubt the very power that will heal."

Years ago, a young journalist interviewed Bonnke David. It was a hostile interview where the journalist was trying to force the direction of the conversation. But she could not corner him. Eventually, she said, "Don't you ever have doubts about your faith and beliefs?" He answered "yes". He did have doubts from time to time, but he always chose to doubt his doubts. Doubt your doubt, and trust God.

We are often so quick to throw weight behind our doubts instead of doubting them and not giving them the attention that they seek. We cannot use our understanding to comprehend the principles of God. It might seem stupid at first, but you will discover eventually, that it amounts to something great. I needed to find a friend because we discussed Christ the last time we met. The conversation was so sweet and engaging that I needed to speak to her again, but I forgot to get her contact information, and by the time I remembered, she had left.

God knew how desperate I wanted to see her again. I was coming back from class one day, and the sun was scorching. My friend asked me to get some groceries with her as we walked together. I never knew it was such a far distance. I got angry and frustrated because I felt my skin burning under the hot sun and my feet hurt from the long walk. On our way home, I saw her! I saw the lady I'd been desperate to find.

Then this thought flashed through my mind: What if I haven't followed her? Even though it was annoying and it got me frustrated, I found the person I had been wanting to meet again. That is how God does His things. It wasn't convenient for me to follow my friend to such a long distance, but finding what I wanted was profitable.

We cannot use our small minds to measure or estimate the power of God. Isaiah 55:8-9: *For my thoughts are not your thoughts, neither are your ways my ways, says the LORD. For as the heavens are higher than the earth, so are my ways higher than your ways, and my thoughts than your thoughts.*

Why is my faith not working?

I have heard many people ask this question. Oftentimes, questions asked include, "But I have faith, I believe but why isn't it working?" I'm glad you will get the answer to that question today, and never stop having faith in God.

Your faith isn't working because it is not solid enough for that situation. It means your faith lacks a macronutrient that will nourish it because it is sick. That nutrient is 'fasting and prayer', to deal with your situation. It is the nutrient required to boost the growth of your malfunctioning faith. See Matthew 17:20-21. *And Jesus said unto them, Because of your unbelief, for verily I say unto you, If you have faith as a grain of mustard seed, you shall say unto this mountain, Remove hence to yonder place, and it shall remove; and nothing shall be impossible for you. Howbeit this kind goeth not out but by prayer and fasting.*

Fasting and prayer repair your faith because when your faith is sick, it cannot fight sickness. The food of faith is prayer. Every man of faith is a prayer warrior. For instance, David O. Oyedepo, Pastor Chris, etc. They are men of prayer.

What can stir up my faith?

This is the next question you need to ask, especially for people with no faith in their hearts but who desire it.

1. The word of God

The word of God is a remedy that can boost your faith, according to the spirit that works in us, which is the spirit of God. Reading the word of God and books about God activates your faith. Romans 10:17: *So then faith cometh by hearing, and hearing by the word of God.*

The Spirit of God gives you a deeper insight into the Word. Whenever you want to read the word of God, you need to do it with the help of the Holy Spirit to show you the deep things in the Word. You can never comprehend the Word without the Holy Spirit.

I had known a particular Bible verse for a long time but never understood what it meant until I asked for the help of the Holy Spirit. I read the verse again and finally caught an understanding. The Bible verse was Romans 1:17: *For therein is the righteousness of God revealed from faith to faith; as it is written, The just shall live by faith.* The understanding I got was that "you will live according to what you believe. If you believe you'd be great, your life will be surrounded by greatness."

So friends, the word of God read through the Spirit of God will boost your faith. A researcher was curious as to why people believe in God or have faith. He began to read books on faith written by great men of God, including the Bible and books on the miracles that God has done, yet he felt nothing. He still couldn't get an answer to the mystery until the Holy Spirit was involved. Here are his words after that encounter.

"I met the pastor of a great church, and we shared our amazement at how the Spirit of the living God was manifesting Himself these days. A big change in my life is the way the scriptures (the word of God) have come alive. It is, of course, the same Bible from which I have always read, but now, it is different. It is different because the Spirit, who inspired those who wrote it, is now inspiring me anew to love and understand it."

Reading the word of God carnally profits nothing. It has to be done with the help of the Holy Spirit, then you will be filled with understanding and start to love the scriptures. The word of God is a sword, with which you can bring down all the fiery darts of the enemy. Ephesian 6:17: *"And take the helmet of salvation and the sword of the Spirit, which is the word of God."*

2.   The presence of God

The presence of God creates an unmatched atmosphere. It fills your entire being with the love of God, and when there is love for God, there is faith. The presence of God fills you with so much hope that you have no choice but to have faith in God.

When I was a kid, I used to be so excited to go to church, and if you ask why, it was because of the indescribable joy I felt in His Presence. This was one of the things that made me have faith in God, and I still do. This kind of presence is only found in God.

His presence will engulf you in His love and increase your love for Him. When you love Him, you will have faith in Him. There was a young man who had no idea what it meant to have faith, but he was a Christian. He was from a family that didn't approve of being a Christian and believing in God. But he was different because he desired to experience what faith was like.

He once believed, but he couldn't explain how it hadn't grown. He blamed it on being a scientist. Some of his colleagues don't believe there is a God because science gives a different perspective about the universe. But somehow, he knew there was something extraordinary, especially when he began to hear testimonies of people being healed by the power of God.

He saw that people got healed by believing that God could heal them. He heard so much about faith that he began to develop an interest in it. He needed to study it and make his discovery about its realness. He had read a lot of Christian books and the latest books on Christian psychology, but still, he lacked the basics that underlay it all — faith.

One day, he meant a man who he never believed should have faith in God. He met him at a church service almost everyone has been talking. He saw that Mr David believed in the Holy Spirit. He then asked himself, If Mr David believed, why then should I be filled with doubts?

When the service began, there was a presence he couldn't describe. He said: "The service began, and I watched in astonishment as the people praised their God with joy and thanksgiving. There seemed to be a presence that pervaded the atmosphere. This 'thing' did not lend itself to analysis. It seemed to saturate their presence with agape love, joy, expectancy (faith), and gladness."

At the end of the service, he became immersed in the love of God. He was boosted with expectancy for God. God's presence is unmatched! Psalms 16:11: *Thou wilt shew me the path of life: in thy presence is fullness of joy; at thy right hand are pleasures for evermore.*

Therefore, use these things to alleviate your faith. For Christians, faith serves as a protective shield in times of trouble. Faith gets you healed; faith revives your being;

and faith gives you boldness. Ephesian 6:16–17: *"Above all, taking the shield of faith, wherewith ye shall be able to quench all the fiery darts of the wicked. And take the helmet of salvation and the sword of the Spirit, which is the word of God."*

Ignorance of healing

Being ignorant of healing prevents a cure. When I say cure, I know what I mean; I have been there before. Some years ago, I was so sick that I couldn't live my life the way I wanted. Even though I was placed on medication, it didn't live up to expectations. Do you know what? I was ignorant of my healing. It took me many years before I could figure it out. It's just like a common proverb: "A person's ignorance is greater than the person himself." This is to say that what you don't know is bigger than you. Until you know it, you are inferior.

This is why a lot of people's healing lies in their ignorance. Sometimes, you don't know the source of your problems or what the solution is or looks like. We tend to be troubled and fearful of the outcome of these things. You recognize when someone is sick because you can tell that he or she is terrified, even though medication has been prescribed.

Most wounds in elderly patients are maintained instead of cured because health professionals lack an understanding of the basic processes that promote healing. Several people have already received healing but are unaware of it.

The spiritual picture presented in the healing of a deaf-mute man (Mark 7:31-37) is of a sinner's moral and spiritual condition. The tongue of the unconverted person is alienated from spiritual truths.

The method that Jesus used for healing this deaf-mute man was unusual. There were few signs of His healings and more explanation on how the healings occurred. Mark revealed the interpretations of Christ's miracles. Some were healed in a crowd, in solitude, by a word, by a touch, or by clay. He healed a few at a time and many more while he was present. Sometimes the healing was immediate, while at other times, it was gradual. Because of His wisdom and omnipotence, God works through Christ as He sees fit.

In this case, Jesus took the man aside from the multitude. It appears that He wanted privacy to avoid any sensation that might arise from unrestrained crowds (Mark 7:33). While away from the interruption of a noisy and pressing throng, the man would be more attentive and receptive. Jesus must awaken a cure and assure the people that he would be healed, it was important. Christ's response to those who brought the deaf-mute man for healing was simply to heal him. Although they dictated the method to use, however, He honoured their faith. He often fulfils His promises in spite of us. However, this is not an excuse for our failures when it comes to healing, but a demonstration of God's grace in showing us favour.

Why are worldly people incapable of assisting those in need?

It was surprising to Christ that the man's friends knew where to take the needy (James 5:13–16). Many in our society recognize the problems of others. They know when a person is mentally and morally sick, but they have no clue as to the cure. Such people are often unaware of their ignorance, resulting in championing strange treatments for people. Instead of leading a person to Christ, pointing them to the Scriptures or biblical passages for solutions, people are likely to take a troubled person to a psychologist or psychiatrist. Unfortunately, worldly advice often perpetuates the problem, rather than solve it. Christ is the answer to the greatest problems and needs of people, for "He is a rewarder of those who diligently seek Him" (Hebrew 11:6)

Why did Jesus put His fingers in the man's ears? Matthew 7:33.

Jesus took him aside to show consideration for the man's feelings about his problematic life. Once they were alone, the first thing Jesus did was to put His fingers into the man's ears. They must be healed if the tongue is to function normally since the man was mute because he could not hear. This symbolic action sent a clear message to the deaf man. It helped to awaken his faith and made him expectant. Besides, we can learn that it is good for us to be alone in God's presence, away from the busy clamour of a confused world, which is not conducive for spiritual reflection (Ecclesiastes 3:7). In the stillness of God's presence, we can build and improve our relationship with Him. Also, individuals need time alone with the Father to keep a focus on Him. *"When you pray, go into your room, and when you have shut your door, pray to your Father who is in secret; and your Father who sees in secret will reward you openly"*, Jesus instructs (Matthew 6:6).

Why did Jesus spit and touch the man's tongue? Mark 7:33.

The common belief at that time was that saliva had medicinal properties. This case and the healing of the blind man at Bethsaida (John 9:6) were the only instances where Jesus used common medical treatments in healing. However, He did not use the saliva for its medicinal purpose, but as a symbol of the power within him. By Christ's touch, the man was shown that the power to heal both his deafness and speech impediment came from Jesus. Even with this, he has to be willing to hear God's words; if not, he would waste the healing and the grace of God (Acts 28:26–28).

This account shows that Jesus did not consider the deaf-mute situation as merely another case, but He saw him as an individual. The man had a special need and a special problem, and with consideration, Jesus dealt with him in a way that spared his feelings and helped him understand.

When the healing became known, the people declared that He has done all things well, which was also God's ruling on His creation. In the beginning, everything was good, but mankind's sins spoiled it. When Jesus came, He brought salvation to the people, He brought the work of spiritual creation, beginning with His church. One day, Christ will bring back God's beauty to the whole world.

What does the Bible say about acknowledging ignorance?

Peter said, "Why do you wonder at this, or why do you stare at us as though by our power or piety we had made him walk?"

The scriptures begin, which we read, including a reference to an "it" and a "him" whom some of us might not recognize. We are fortunate to have a beautiful stained-glass window depicting him and it, right on the wall of the sanctuary. Take a look at it as you come up to communion because it is hard to see from the nave of the church; it will be on your right as you approach the altar rail. It depicts Peter and John standing before the man at the Beautiful Gate of the temple. He is the "he," and the "it" is his miraculous healing through the name of Jesus.

One day, Peter and John were going up to the temple at the hour of prayer, and a man lame from birth was being carried in. People would lay him outside daily at the gate of the temple, called the Beautiful Gate, so that he could ask for alms from those entering the temple. When he saw Peter and John, he asked them for alms. Peter looked intently at him, as did John, and said, "Look at us." He fixed his attention on them, expecting to receive something from them. But Peter said, "I have no silver or gold, but what I have, I give you; in the name of Jesus of Nazareth, stand up and walk."

He took him by the right hand and raised him up, and immediately his feet and ankles were made strong. And jumping up, he stood and began to walk, and he entered the temple with them, walking and leaping and praising God. All the people saw him walking and praising God, and they recognized him as the one who used to sit and ask for alms, and they were filled with wonder, amazed at what happened to him. Acts 3:1-10.

That's the "it" and the "him". Our reading continues with Peter's testimony to the crowd that was amazed by this; that it was the power of Jesus' name that wrought the miracle. He castigated the people and their rulers for having rejected and killed the author of life. He testified that he and the apostles were witnesses to the resurrection of God's chosen and righteous one, in whose name and by whose name the man was healed. He called them to repent, even though, he says they "acted in ignorance".

The next ignorance addressed by Peter follows. He accused the people of rejecting Jesus and choosing a murderer to be released instead when Pilate was ready to let Him go. But as Peter continued, they and their rulers acted in ignorance; an ignorance that, in its ironic way, helped fulfil God's promise that the Messiah would suffer.

However, now that the suffering was over and Christ has been raised from the dead, the school of God was back in session: it was time to learn something new, of which they were once ignorant. It was time for them to put the ignorance behind them, become informed of the gospel, and embrace the truth of the power in Jesus' name, not just to heal a disabled man but to restore them all to the wholeness that God intends for everyone through grace and faith.

The first epistle of John also addressed two forms of ignorance: the world is ignorant of God and of us as children of God, but we also are not without our limitations. As John says, "We are God's children now; what we will be has not yet been revealed." There is more to learn, more revelations to come, and more opening of the eyes of our faith.

The good news is that our ignorance is not total: "What we do know", he writes, "is this: when he is revealed, we will be like him, for we will see him as he is." We don't see Him yet, but when we do, we will be like Him. We will learn something new and wonderful. This is the hope of all who seek Jesus, who count themselves among those who believe in His name and are washed in His blood and are united with Him in death that we may be united with Him in the resurrection. Presently, as St. Paul also affirmed, our knowledge is partial, like a dim mirror. But when Christ is revealed, we shall know as we are known, fully informed and fully enlightened by the light of the world, the revelation of the Son of God.

It is fitting that the last ignorance we are presented with is that of the apostles themselves. They heard the testimony of Peter and the disciples who encountered

Jesus on the way to Emmaus. While they were arguing and trying to understand all that happened, Jesus appeared among them to their amazement and, in the case of some, disbelief.

And Jesus, ever the good teacher, instructed them gently. He relieved their ignorance with the good news and reminded them of what he had told them beforehand; before they came to Jerusalem, before the time He said He would suffer; and that all of these were attested in the scriptures (in the Law of Moses, in the Prophets, and the Psalms) they had read all their lives and knew by heart. Remember that the experience matched the promise. They needed a good teacher to inform them of how the promises of the past became real in the present.

This is the way God continues to enlighten us, lift our ignorance, and inform our minds. Not suddenly, but bit by bit, story by story, revelation by revelation. He does it through His promises; poetry and prose; repeating the lesson until we understand; words from on high; hopes whispered into our hearts; and through the groaning of the Spirit within us. The good teacher teaches and the great physician heals.

May we, like the man at the gate, reach out for what we do not know but find ourselves grasping the hand of the

One who brings us gifts better than what we can ask for
or imagine; even Jesus Christ, our Lord.

CHAPTER NINE

HEALING IS A CHOICE

I call heaven and earth to record this day against you, that I have set before you life and death, blessing and cursing: therefore choose life, that both thou and thy seed may live. Deuteronomy 30:19

The Lord has placed healing and ways (a blueprint) to get healed before you. Therefore, it is your choice to choose life. God wishes to make that choice for you, but He cannot because He has given man the free will to choose, the way He gave Adam the choice of the tree of life and the tree of death.

It is your decision to make.

God has set before us life and death, health and sickness. The choice is yours. Many Christians are victims of this and wonder why God hasn't healed them or why God is healing others but not them. The difference between who is getting healed and who is not is a word: "choice". They decided to allow God to heal them.

Let me make this clear: God has given you everything you need to rebuke sickness, fear, and the devil. He has given us His Son, His name, the Holy Spirit, His anointing, and His word. He has given us everything!

Jesus Christ said, "It is finished!" Everything has been given to us, but if you choose not to pick any of these, God will let you die. Yes, it might seem harsh, but it is the truth. God cannot choose for you. He has done His part; it is your turn to do yours.

At a mall, I heard a woman preaching about how God healed her of a certain disease when she was on the verge of death. It was a great testimony, but a man suddenly approached her aggressively. He said, "Why did God heal you and not my wife?" He said it once, and the woman blinked a couple of times with no answer for him.

She said nothing, so he repeated, "Why did God heal you and not my wife?" He almost pushed her off her feet, but she stood firm. When she finally spoke, she said "I don't know. God is the healer. Why wouldn't He heal your wife?"

His eyes were teary; he looked hurt, and the woman felt guilty for sharing her testimony with others.

Here is the thing; until you decide to choose life, God cannot do anything for you. God is a God of His words. He has given us His word to decide for ourselves and He would never go back on His word. God cannot change His word; they are unchangeable forever. Because He says, "My words will I not break". Psalm 89:34 says; *My covenant will I not break, nor alter the thing that is gone out of my lips.* Also in Isaiah 55:11; *So shall my word be that goeth forth out of my mouth: it shall not return unto me void, but it shall accomplish that which I please, and it shall prosper in the thing whereto I sent it.*

Hence, God cannot be moved by emotions but by faith. He says, "Have faith in me; I have given you what to use to destroy that sickness. Just have faith in me." He is a God beyond reproach. Your tears will not make Him go back on His words. All you need to do is to use the ways He has given you to cure your sickness through faith.

When God said in Deuteronomy 30 to make your choice, Satan was aware of it. The attack from the devil is determined by your choice. Satan comes in when you let him. Every man was given a choice on how to live at birth. He could either choose Jesus or the world, Jesus or death, or Jesus or a sick body. God has given man the privilege of choice.

This is why He can never force us to serve Him. He gave us the choice; no man is forced.

Mark 10:47–51 says, *And when he heard that it was Jesus of Nazareth, he began to cry out and say, Jesus, thou Son of David, have mercy on me. And many charged him that he should hold his peace; but he cried the more a great deal, Thou son of David, have mercy on me. And Jesus stood still, and commanded him to be called. And they call the blind man, saying unto him, Be of good comfort; rise; he calleth thee.*

And he, casting away his garment, rose and came to Jesus. And Jesus answered and said unto him, What will you that I should do unto you? The blind man said unto him, Lord, that I might receive my sight.

Jesus knew what he wanted, but was waiting for him to make his choice by asking.

Jesus knows what we want, but He wants us to express our expectations. So it is our choice to ask God to heal us, even though God is ready to get us healed. Do not assume; ask. God is aware of our desires, but He still awaits our requests.

Therefore, choose to embrace God's word and His healing. You are making that decision today! Today is your day to get healed. No more lies from the devil. You have a father who is a healer!

CHAPTER TEN

PROOF THAT GOD CAN HEAL YOU

God never assures you of something without providing proof. He always leaves proof to make you believe that He can truly heal. God always leaves proof. Acts 14:17: *"Yet he did not leave himself without some witness [as evidence of himself], in that he kept constantly doing good things and showing you kindness and giving you rains from heaven and fruitful seasons, filling your hearts with food and happiness."* He has assured you of good health; therefore, He gives you proof.

Here are testimonies of God's healing. Some people think God chooses to heal or not to heal. It is wrong. Why will He choose not to heal you when it hurts Him to see you sick? God will never choose not to heal His children when they call upon Him for healing. He is not a biased God. He has the desire to heal anyone who trusts in His healing.

Every Sunday, the most exciting thing about the church service is the testimony period. I love to listen to testimonies because it shows how great the God I serve is.

HEALED FROM EPILEPSY

I suffered from epilepsy for two years. It all started at my workplace. The first day I fainted, I was rushed to a nearby hospital. I was examined, and the doctor said I was fine without discovering what was wrong or the reason I had fainted. Since the doctor's report says nothing is wrong, I went back to work, even though my wife wasn't convinced. I told her I was fine and kissed her goodbye before I left.

I worked perfectly fine that day, but the next day I didn't know what was happening to me again. I fainted and hit my head on the steel I was working on. This time, my wife was informed immediately, and I was taken to the same hospital which said nothing was wrong with me. Luckily, it was a different doctor who attended to me, and he found out that I had been injured in the fall.

I ran to the room I was placed in. When I gained consciousness, I saw her crying, and that destabilized me. We've been married for a long time and have never been seriously ill. This was the first time that I had fainted, and no reason could be pinpointed.

The doctor said he was going to examine me for a few days, so I had to be admitted to the hospital. I was given a break from my work, and my wife refused to leave my side. She stayed with me during the admission. It was for four days; I fainted again across the lobby to my room on the second day, and my wife screamed to get a nurse to assist.

I didn't know what was wrong, but I wasn't feeling like I should. I knew something was wrong; I wasn't feeling well. I wonder what happened to me all of a sudden—where was this coming from?

When the doctor came with the report, he said I had epilepsy and I was shocked, with my wife as well, because we have never experienced such since we've been together. The doctor said it was epilepsy, and it wasn't getting better with the drugs I was given. I kept getting worse, fainting more frequently than before, and we were getting scared.

We didn't know what to do because the doctor's prescriptions weren't working, including the herbs that my wife's mother asked me to take. None of them was working. I began to cry all night, asking what was wrong with me and wondering if I had been bewitched. It must be.

Then one day a friend of mine came to visit me at home; I had been discharged and couldn't go to work because I wasn't fine yet and the situation had worsened. His name was Mike. He told me what I was going through might not be ordinary and that I shouldn't be scared because I have someone who can heal me. I asked him who, and he said, "Jesus Christ. He can heal you; it doesn't matter what it is. Be it ordinary or not. He is the master of extraordinary."

I knew a little about Christ, but I had never witnessed anything like His miraculous healing. I asked him, "How is it done? And what can I do to get me healed by Jesus?" He said, "Just ask. He is always ready to heal you." He gave me a warm smile, and from his green eyes, I could see he was honest and had faith that Jesus could heal me of epilepsy.

I appreciated his advice. So my wife and I agreed to try God's healing since all the drugs and herbs were making things worse. The next Sunday, we were in church, and I opened my heart to Jesus to let Him heal me.

As the service started, the choir began to sing, the music and voices were so pleasant. They were giving glory to

God, and there was this joy and sweetness in the air. As the atmosphere was so beautiful and pleasant, something told me to ask now. I asked God to heal me of this epilepsy because I was not okay. I don't want to be sick, and I don't even want to see my wife cry because of me.

I opened my mouth and said, "Dear God, I know you can heal me of this illness. I believe in your power; my friend said you are the master of the extraordinary. Please, do something extraordinary in my life and health. In Jesus' name, Amen." I prayed, and my heart felt renewed and free like that of a baby. I felt like something had taken all my worries away.

Then, in a few minutes, I felt a cold. It was pleasant, as if something had hit me and brought me back to life. Honestly, I began to feel different and was no longer miserable.

I screamed next to my wife, who was already seeing the changes in my expression. "Linda, I think I have been healed just now. I feel entirely different."

There were tears in her eyes, as she cried, "Glory be to God! I knew He would heal you. Thank you, Jesus!" This was how I was healed. It was miraculous, and if I hadn't experienced it myself, I wouldn't believe it. But now, I believe in Jesus!

-MASTI MAGA

HEALED FROM BREAST CANCER

God is God!

When I was a young boy, my mother was diagnosed with breast cancer. She had several hard lumps in each breast, confirmed by an x-ray, and was scheduled for a double mastectomy. As she was being wheeled down the hallway to the operating room, she began to think of her sons, my brother and me. She knew if she died, there would be no one to teach me and my brother the ways of the Lord. In desperation, she cupped her breasts in her hands and cried out to God to heal her.

Suddenly she felt warmth and a sensation of electricity in her breasts, and she instantly knew God had healed her. Nevertheless, the nurses prepared her for surgery, but before the doctor cut her, they discovered that they could no longer detect the lumps in her breasts. They delayed the surgery and sent her back for more X-rays. They could find no lumps, so they cancelled the surgery.

Though the lumps were gone, she still felt weary and sick, and she got worse day by day. A second diagnosis was given; leukaemia, confirmed by blood tests.

Whatever treatment the doctors were giving her at that time was ineffective, and her life force was draining away. Near death, she had a dream where she encountered Jesus. Many years later, she could still recall the events, the scents, the presence of Jesus, and an intimate conversation with our Lord.

She did not want to return to her cancer-ridden body, yet she knew she must, and she did. But her body was not healed. Wearily, she dragged herself to her car and drove to her friend, Joan's house. Joan said she looked more dead than alive and asked her if she wanted to live. Though conflicted, Mom answered yes.

Joan laid her hands on her and prayed for her loudly and in tongues, commanding her healing in the name of Jesus. Again, my mom felt warmth and something like a body, and she knew she was healed. This time, she was. All the glory belongs to God!

- MICHAEL GALIEY

I BELIEVE IN JESUS

I believe in Jesus; He has heard my request. Thank you for everything, Jesus. For those who are reading this, I know it's long, but it was worse to experience a disease no one knows, and it was wonderful to know and experience Jesus. Overall, the journey with Jesus has been joyous. Jesus loves you more than you can ever imagine. He is so kind. He gave Himself on the cross for us. So, have faith; there is hope that you will find peace; believe in the word and Him.

- IRENE WEST

HEALED FROM A HEART ATTACK

Last year I had a friend who, at the age of 28 (a few days before his birthday), had a heart attack and was left on the ground at his job for almost 40 minutes. He technically died. His heart stopped. Then the doctor performed surgery on him, and he was in a coma for about 2 weeks.

That doctor said that if he came out of the coma, he would be too weak because no one has ever come out of one and resumed a normal life. Every day, there were chain prayers and multiple visits to his hospital room, where we prayed and sang praises to God because we knew He is a miracle worker. Just as in the Bible, when Jesus raised a child from the dead, He could do it again because He is the same, yesterday, today, and forever.

One day, he woke up and was able to speak; he had his full memory but was weak. He was also able to move. Today, he turned 30; he was able to see his children. He walks, talks, and works as if it never happened. The doctors said, I don't know to whom you are praying, but this is a miracle. I witnessed acts of the Bible in the modern day. God raised him from the dead and healed him. If He did it for my friend, He can do it for you or any of your loved ones! Thank you, Jesus.

- ALEXANDRIA NORTON

HEALED FROM A STRANGE PET IN HIS EARS

I am 70 years old now. I was raised as a Christian but followed God loosely as a youth. I decided to make God a priority in my life at about the age of 23. A year later, I was living in the mountains with pets and farm animals. I was asleep one night when something entered my left ear. I tried as much as possible to take it out, but I couldn't.

It periodically made noise, like a person eating celery. If I poked at it, the noise would stop momentarily. I asked my wife to put her ear next to mine and see if she could hear it. Yes, she could. Living on a tight budget and without insurance, I dreaded the thought of paying for a doctor. There was no pain, but after two days of this, it was beginning to bother me. I began to get troubled about the pet in my ear that had refused to leave and it caused me great discomfort.

I continued to work as a mechanic at a local shop. While working, the sound would come and go (an annoying sound). I would go into the restroom and try to make it stop by poking and flushing with water. After one of these duals in the bathroom, a thought came to me as I walked back into the shop area. "I don't need to let this worry me; I am God's child. It's His problem to take care of my pains." Immediately, three things happened.

The noise in my ears went away (forever).

I saw shimmering images of blue, gold, red, and iridescent highlights coming out like heat waves; cars, buildings, streets, everything.

I felt the most perfect peace, impossible to compare with anything.

From what I remember, it lasted about 10–15 minutes, and then the sights and feelings slowly faded for another 10 minutes or so. One strange thing was that I worked with 4-5 others in this small shop. None of them were present when this happened. I know it was God's healing. I have seen God's miraculous hand in my life for many years. I can't wait to hold him!

- LAWRENCE

HEALED FROM RIGHT HIP INFLAMMATION

My right hip and thigh hurt for about six months. It was painful to bend, sit, and lie down. I have been on a muscle relaxer and a lidocaine patch, but they did not help at all. On November 6, 2021, the pain from the inflammation was so bad that I wanted to tell my husband to take me to emergency care, but then I called upon God and repeated His words.

He spoke to me in my dreams many years ago, saying that all my enemies have been defeated, no exception—that pain and inflammation have been defeated. I cried due to the horrible pain and inflammation while holding onto God's words and promises.

All of a sudden, brethren, I felt peace and calmness in my body. I sat down quietly throughout the evening because this happened late in the afternoon. The following day, there was no pain or inflammation. I began to thank God, but I did not tell my family members yet.

One week later, no pain; I bent thrice and walked up and down the stairs, yet no pain. I then told my family members what God had done for me, and they rejoiced with me. Before, I was in so much pain, I could not sit, bend, or walk up and down stairs without experiencing pain. God is amazing! God is faithful!

He keeps His words and promises. God does not lie. God took away my pain and inflammation. Trust and hold on to God's words. Please join me in thanking God for His mercies, compassion, goodness, and faithfulness. To God almighty be all the glory!

- GODGIVE

HEALED FROM THE COVID-19 VIRUS

I want to share a testimony of how God healed my tendon with less than a mustard seed of faith. I was diagnosed with COVID-19 a few months ago through a rapid blood test. I had it bad at one stage; my chest closed. I battled to breathe and could not move my chest because of the lack of oxygen in my limbs. I got pins and needles in my fingers and feet.

I had no sense of smell or taste, my body was sore and my throat was irritated. I almost did not see 2021, but once again through faith, I asked my fiancé to contact my pastor to pray for me over the phone, and after that, my chest cleared up so I could breathe. After my isolation, I had an infection called COVID pneumonia, and my chest closed up again, so I once again thought that I was not going to make it.

This time, I was scared because my fiancé was not at home and my voice was gone. I know that I try to live righteously, but the thought went through my mind; "Are you ready to meet the Father?" Deep inside, I feel I could and should have done more to have a closer relationship with God. I also realized then that I was going to die without saying goodbye or making amends. I knew I do forgive the people who hurt me oftentimes, especially my family. I decided that I was going to fight the inevitable.

I sent a message to my pastor, asking him to pray for me in the name of Jesus, and once again, through faith, my chest opened up and I began to breathe. After that, I had blood tests done and ended up with blood clots, but Jesus came through for me. I am back at work and getting stronger every day. I spend every second telling everyone that God is real. He is still doing miracles, and we need to put our trust in Him; He will never leave us nor forsake us.

We need to praise him even in the storm, no matter what you go through in life. Sometimes, things happen for a reason; they are there to make you stronger so that you can handle any obstacle that comes your way and trust God. I have learned to put everything in God's hands, and then everything will fall into place. He is the provider; He is a miracle worker and does not expect too much from us. All He wants is for us to confess our sins, believe that His Son died for us on the cross, and have a close relationship with Him.

The Book of Revelation is being fulfilled as we speak. It is important to plead the blood of Jesus over yourself and your family and to put on the whole armour of God. Please share the testimony of my healing so that people will know that God is faithful and good, and all we need to do is call His name. And He will be there. Cast your anxieties on Him. He will give you rest; let Him lead you, and He will direct your steps.

- ANJA

RESCUED FROM AN INCIDENT

My baby and I fell in the bathroom. He hit his head so hard, and I became devastated. He was crying so much, and I started to cry as well because, as a mother, I could feel the pain my baby was going through. I did not know what to do, and I did not want to inform my husband about it. Then I called on the merciful God to make my baby okay. He heard and answered my prayers; my baby was healthy with no injuries. He is walking, talking, and eating well. I know that God rescued him; he would not have been well without God.

- ALICIA

RESCUED FROM ALCOHOLISM

Jesus reached the bottom to save me. I was an alcoholic, and it has been 27 years now without a drink because the Lord saved me. Then he called me to preach the gospel, and I have been doing so for 27 years now. Satan has tried everything to destroy me. I lost my family through a divorce after I broke down with a bad spinal cord disease. I died once, but the Lord brought me back. The doctor could not cure my illness; it was one of the most painful conditions, and the doctor had me on all kinds of medications.

I found out my wife was walking out on me after 20 years of marriage. She backslid from God. So I went through the divorce; the church turned its back on me and would not let me preach. One night, my illness got so bad that I was ready to be taken to the hospital, but they were praying for me. So I told God that night to either heal me or take me to heaven because I could not go on due to the intense pain, despite the pain medications the doctor had me on.

Finally, one night at a church of a pastor I knew, I was prayed for, and God healed me; praise the Lord forever! The Lord brought a good Christian lady into my life; we got married, and today, I am back to preaching in the church that told me I should never preach again because of my divorce. I am thankful to God for the restoration of everything that I lost. Thank you, Jesus!

- ROBERT

HEALED FROM AN UNKNOWN TERRIBLE SICKNESS

I was sixteen years old when my life changed overnight. I was a healthy, intelligent, and bright teenager who suddenly lost mobility, unable to walk, think, or make decisions independently. Weeks turned into months, and my condition worsened, taking its toll on my family's work life and finances. They now have to care for me full-time.

I spent the next five years in and out of the hospital; doing tests, scans, treatments, MRIs, X-rays, ECGs, blood tests, and drug trials, all in an attempt to find the cause of the condition. Doctors could see the physical damage going on, but they could not find the underlying cause of it. Having a serious health condition that cannot be diagnosed by doctors makes you feel like a walking question mark. There is no closure. How can you find treatment for a problem that no one else can see?

In mid-2017, we found a facility in Germany that deals with specialized testing for diseases. I had a full range done, and my result came back positive for Lyme disease. My markers were high, and it showed my immune system was being suppressed by this disease. Lyme disease is an infectious disease caused by the bacteria *Borrelia burgdorferi*, which can be transmitted to humans by a bite from an infected black-legged deer tick.

The tick becomes infected after feeding on an infected deer, bird, or mouse. Many people with Lyme disease have no memory of a tick bite. During the initial 3-30 days period of infection, you may or not notice something amiss. Symptoms range from obvious signs to subtle ones and none at all. You may develop a fever, headache, chills, and swollen lymph nodes. You may feel fatigued or have muscle and joint aches. You may develop the characteristics of a bulls-eye rash, which in medical terms is called erythema migrants (EM), or you may not.

After eight years without correctional treatment, I now had chronic late-stage Lyme disease and neuroborreliosis (LNB), where the disease started affecting the nervous system. During this period, I was 21 years old. My menstrual cycle stopped. I developed a gallbladder infection, and a scan revealed that I had gallstones and a hiatus hernia. I was also diagnosed with pernicious anaemia and polycystic ovarian syndrome. I became underweight and severely weak; I experienced severe headaches and neck stiffness, as well as painful inflammation in my eye.

I lost my distance vision, had facial palsy, nerve pain, shooting pains, numbness, arthritis with severe joint pain and swellings, particularly on the knees and other large joints, intermittent pain in tendons, muscles, joints, and bones, heart palpitations, night sweats, and vomiting. I could not list the full extent of the disfigurement, but my family would tell you that it was horrific.

The following two years were spent travelling across the country to private clinics. The drives were long, sometimes 6-7 hours for an hourly appointment. None of the treatments worked, and I was deemed treatment-resistant and incurable. After eight years, I decided that I would stop seeking further treatment and accept my condition.

I began to question why I was born and I wanted to end my life. Why was I existing, and what was the meaning of my life? I was raised in a non-religious home, and no one had explained to me that there was a meaning to life, so I had no reason to question that until now.

I looked at the train station across the road, and in my mind, with tears down my face, I cried out, "God, if you exist, where are you?" I wanted to walk in front of the train.

I was standing on the side of the street, and as I turned to look, one of the missionary evangelists spotted me. He walked up to me, placed his hand on my shoulder, and said to me, "I know what you are going through." At that moment, I felt his hand fill my body with peace.

I looked into this man's eyes and said, "What is that in your eyes?" I could barely get my words out. "That's the Lord Jesus," he replied. "What are you doing tonight at 7 p.m.?" he asked. "Nothing, why?" "We are having a healing night in our church tonight; you should come."

The incurable disease was cured. I went to the church that night and was told that I could have a relationship with Jesus Christ and that He had a plan for my life. It was then that the Lord began to reveal His love to me, and I gave my life to Him. I was baptized one month later and began to read the Bible and attend the meetings. I vowed that I would turn away from my old life. As I prayed, He spoke and told me He was going to deliver and heal me. I trusted what I had heard and never gave up on believing that I would be free from the disease.

When I attended church, others would walk up to me, lay hands on me, and pray for healing. Months passed, and I saw my symptoms disappearing without treatment; in early 2019, I was completely delivered from the disease. I am now 26 years old, and my organs are functioning normally. I am independent and have my own house. I love animals and enjoy walking in nature. I am re-building a life I never thought possible because of the restoration of God.

If He can do it for me, He can do it for you!

-Amy McLeod

A BROKEN PELVIS HEALED!

Three days before Thanksgiving, my daughter and I decided to go horseback riding. While warming the horses in our arena, I was thrown by my young horse. I knew it was serious because I couldn't move and the pain was excruciating. After X-rays and a CAT scan, they discovered I had separated my pelvis from front to back along with internal injuries.

After a few days in the ICU and some time in recovery, I was back home and on the mend. With the help of physical therapy, I was back on my feet within six weeks. All seemed to be going well, but the pain in my hips began to increase. At three months, I could barely walk, and the pain was unbearable.

I went for more X-rays, and an MRI showed that my pelvis had become unstable, it was separating again and putting pressure on my hip joints. My orthopaedic surgeon's idea was screwed, along with the risk that it might not relieve the pain and could break when I'm active. None of the options sound good, so I became depressed and felt defeated. My wife and I began to pray.

God had a better plan; I just didn't know it yet. My friend, James, came over to my shop to shoe my horse and realized how painful it was for me to stand to keep the horse calm. He mentioned that his friend, Bruce Carlson, was in town and that he had prayed for people like me, and God healed them. He wondered if I would be interested in visiting him and seeing what God would do.

I met them at his ranch. I shared with Bruce what had happened and how my pelvis shifted and separated as I tried to move, and how the pain was so bad, I was barely able to walk, sit, or stand. He said to have a seat right here in this straight-back chair. Bruce took and held the heels of my feet in his hands, and the three of us could see that the right one was an inch or so shorter than the other (pelvic out of alignment).

Bruce began to pray, taking God's words as true and trusting Christ would do as He promised. As he prayed, I saw with my eyes the right heel grew out, passed the other, and then came back to the same length as the left. "God is putting your pelvis back in alignment", Bruce explained. He asked me to stand, and laid his hands on my hips again, believing in Christ and His word for the power of feeling.

This time, I could feel someone squeezing the SI joints together. When Bruce had finished praying for me, I could tell that something was different. Still in pain, I went on, and that day was a Thursday. Friday morning, I woke up with not as much pain, and I was able to be on my feet much longer. By Sunday (this is not a joke), I was throwing horseshoes with my boys pain-free. I loaded and unloaded three moving trucks, and I've been on the go ever since. I thank my Lord Jesus Christ and His faithful servant Bruce Carlson for this miracle of healing. Truly, God is the one who heals.

- BRIAN HILLS

A SAMPLE OF GOD'S HANDWORK

We know that the biggest miracle we will ever see is someone receiving Jesus as their saviour. Plus, it is the only one that has eternal value. We pray that there are people who receive salvation at every meeting we hold. We also pray for signs and miracles that will point people to the one true God who loves them and can truly set the captives free.

We receive several calls a day from people who want us to pray for them, but please, remember that Jesus is the healer. We are just people who are in love with God and have no more privileged access to Him than anybody else. Anyone who wants to have a relationship with Him can pray and know that He is listening to them because He loves us. The Bible tells us in James 4:7, *"Come near to God, and He will come near to you."*

A Miracle Done by Jesus in the Church: "After hearing your testimony at Jings Fire Church a few years ago, you prayed for me over a creative miracle for my throat. I had two surgeries to remove two masses. In the final surgery, they removed the middle section of my hyoid bone so it won't grow back again, and they removed a portion of the back of my tongue that connects to the bone. This anchors everything around your voice box.

After that surgery, I had problems with swallowing; I was barely able to eat, and there was no hope of a cure. And worst of all, the deepest hurt was no longer having the ability to sing, and even reading books to my children was painful. The doctor said there was no cure and they would have to 'dream up' a surgery to help me function. I was in constant pain and could barely eat. I was frozen with fear.

I desperately needed a creative miracle. What man said was not possible, God said otherwise. I was healed that night. You prayed for a creative miracle in my throat and for bones to grow, and the enemy was trying to silence me from leading worship. Since that night, I am back to singing and playing the guitar at my church, while sharing with others how I have been healed to sing again with no swallowing issues. Thank you for sharing your powerful testimony, which led to me receiving creative healing as well. And thank you, Jesus, for your powerful healing!"

- JOE MARCUS

CANCER IS CURED WITHOUT THE USE OF ANY MEDICINE, ONLY GOD!

I worked for the Department of Corrections for 30 years as a teacher and had just retired. Right after my retirement, I noticed blood in my urine and was diagnosed with stage 2 bladder cancer with very aggressive cancerous cells. I was advised by my doctor to have a total removal of my bladder and prostrate within two weeks because the cancer was extremely aggressive

I was told the surgery would take 8–9 hours, with a 6–8 months recovery period. I had a large tumour in my bladder, and it had spread into the muscle tissue, and the prostrate had cancer as well. My brother and his close friend met me one morning for breakfast, and Bruce Van Natta came with them to pray for me. My brother told me about Bruce's story, so I was excited to meet him.

After we finished eating, Bruce asked if he could lay his hands on me and pray. Bruce lifted his shirt and showed me his scars after sharing his incredible story. I sat there as Bruce anointed me with oil and prayed right there amongst everyone in the restaurant. I didn't feel anything special happen right then and there; however, that evening and into the next day, I felt vibrations going on in my body, especially in my lower extremities where the cancer was located. It felt strange.

For the next couple of months, I began to feel better. I also changed my diet and started eating well, but I knew something was different. On January 5th, I went to the University of Wisconsin Hospital in Madison for a second opinion and to be retested by an oncology specialist. That morning, I took a blood and urine test, followed by a consultation with experts specializing in bladder cancer. I was told that they had reviewed all my reports from my doctors in Green Bay.

It was their consensus that it was in my best interest to pursue the recommendation of my doctor in Green Bay and immediately have the surgery. I was also told that I could forgo the hurtful retest based on the previous reports, and because it was a very aggressive cancer, they were anxious to do surgery and chemotherapy. I insisted that they scope my bladder again just to make sure.

This is where it gets really interesting. During the test, the doctor scoped my bladder and then called another doctor in to take a look. After 15 minutes, he called in a third doctor, who, while scoping, kept whispering to the others. After the procedure, they told me that because it was so late in the day, they would come to me the next day with the results.

The following day, I was informed by the specialist that the options we discussed yesterday were still open, but he went on to say that my bladder looked good and there was no cancer there now; my urine had no traces of blood or bacteria; and that it was their consensus that I wouldn't need the surgery based on their new observations. The tumour was gone. They suggested I still consider chemotherapy and radiation as precautionary measures because of cancer that was originally there but had now vanished. I said no way; I know what chemotherapy and radiation do to the body.

It has been a year, and I feel the best I have ever felt in my life. By changing my diet and eating healthy, I have now lost 50 lbs. Everyone comments on how good I look and how great my skin looks. My blood pressure is in a normal range, and my cholesterol and sugar levels are normal as well. During one of my tests, they said I had the arteries and blood of a 25-year-old!

I thank God for His great healing. I am forever blessed and grateful, and one fact I do know is that God heals.

- BRAD HENTGES

EYES HEALED

A few years ago, I was buffeted by an unusual eye condition that doctors could not explain or treat. Unable to look to the left or right, wearing dark glasses indoors, and being forced to keep blinds closed even on overcast days, reading was almost impossible because of how the condition affected my eye function.

What was worse was that I was to take a two-day medical board exam with hundreds of questions, which required pouring through volumes of books to prepare. It wasn't just textbooks; I couldn't read any text without stopping after a few lines. I was in the middle of applying for a residency job that had already been delayed for a while, and everything was at a standstill because of this anomalous eye disorder.

Doctors seemed to think it might be related to an autoimmune illness called Hashimoto's disease, which I had, but after extensive testing, they still could not give me a definitive diagnosis. At a loss for what to do, only the Lord could help me with this problem. I worked up the nerve to contact the ministry, where Brother Bruce was kind enough to pray over my eye issue, my difficult job situation, as well as my finances.

I also requested prayers about attending the Bay Revival, as my family were against my interest in it. Within days, a job opportunity emerged, and a week later, after Brother Van Natta prayed a second time over the phone, I picked up the Bible and was immediately able to read without stopping. I was able to resume studying and eventually, completed my exam.

Since that time, I've had the chance to attend Bay Revival three times and I've had the privilege of attending other Christian meetings in my area. There has been a breakthrough in healing, miraculous doors opening, and household financial growth. My parents have even gone back to church after 25 years of not attending. There is power in His word, and He hears our prayers. Don't give up because God is right around the corner with the healing that you need!

- W.N

TAILBONE HEALED

Tail Bone healed after 30 years of affliction.

I got a call today from Vickey Coates; she came to our church last year regularly. She is now going to another church because her family goes there, and they pressured her to go where they go, but she wanted to be with us and also be with her family too. She tells people to come to our church when they want a deeper experience with the Lord. She sent someone to us recently and wanted to inform us and give us the lady's name.

So, we talked, and in our conversation, she told me that she was at our church when Bruce ministered a year ago when Pastor Dar and I were out of town. She said she was healed when you prayed for her, Bruce. She had injured her tailbone when giving birth to her son 30 years ago, and it had caused severe pain ever since then. It hurt for her to even sit down on a chair. That pain left, and she was completely healed—no more pain! She was healed for the first time in 30 years. She is in her 50s, and it has now been closed to a year since you prayed for her, and the pain has not come back.

- CLARA KOBS

ARTHRITIS HEALED

I was diagnosed with rheumatoid arthritis about 14 years ago. I was in extreme pain from my neck down to my toes. After going to the doctor for some time, I was given methotrexate, which is a medication for cancer, but it helped take away the pain. I could function while I was on it. Over the years, I had attempted to go off the medications several times, but within a couple of weeks, I was in so much pain that I had to take them again.

Then I met Bruce, and he prayed over me. I went off the meds once again and was pain-free for about six months, but then the symptoms returned. He said, "Teri, why did you not call me and let me know how you were feeling?" Then he said that I was allowing the devil to take away my healing and that I had to have faith that God is the great healer. So once he prayed for me again, I went off my medications. And now it has been two years since I have been healed!

I went to my doctor for my annual physical, and as she gave me my results, she asked if I had an RA. I said, "No, not any more. I do not have RA." She said that was not what my results said. A normal count is 10, and she said I was 332. I know what 332 feels like; that was my count when I was first diagnosed and I could hardly move.

I told her I had never felt so good and that I was going to believe what my body was telling me and that God had healed me. Later, I thought, why would God allow my count to be so high? Then I realized that if the count were normal, they would say I was misdiagnosed. But with the count saying I have it—RA—and my body not feeling any pain, it proves my God is the great physician, and He has healed me.

I will continue to give praise and glory to Jesus Christ and His Word for healing me. It shows how much He loves us all, and all we need to do is put our faith in Him alone. Not drugs, not the doctor, but Him!

- TERI CERNOCH

BIPOLAR OVERCAME BY HIS LOVE

I am from South Africa and was raised in a Christian family. I gave my life to Christ when I was 12 years old. The environment in which I grew up, my family situation, and the emotional instability in my house led to my going out of balance.

I would sit on the roof of the house during arguments and pray. When I was about 17 or 18, I started struggling emotionally. I tied the emotional struggles to circumstances based on how I perceived them. I was a missionary in Swaziland by the time I was 19. At the end of that, I had a complete mental breakdown. I got a bottle of painkillers and drank them all with soda.

The people around me realized something was wrong, and they took me to the hospital. After that, they sent me to counsellors, but nothing seemed to work, so I had to go home. That was disappointing to me because I had given everything to God and wanted to help people. I worked for a company for the next seven years before being diagnosed with bipolar disorder in September 2018.

I saw various psychologists and tried medications, but nothing seemed to work. Most of the time, I was depressed, but when I went manic, I would spend all my money and go delusional and irrational. Back then. I thought I had to be perfect and polished when I appeared before the throne of God, so I looked for things to make me okay.

I tried everything. Later, I got involved in using drugs (I have been clean for seven years now). I thought God was angry, distant and disappointed in me. I felt He would reject me if I tell Him what I was going through. I felt like a disappointment every time I woke up from my coma. My father was emotionally absent, so it was hard to relate to a heavenly Father.

My mom prayed for me; she is a strong woman, and at some point, the doctor told me two-thirds of my liver was not functioning. My sister was pregnant at the time; she pushed me and said, "What are you doing with your life?" At that time, my family did not want me around because I was not healthy. Hey, they loved me, but they needed to take care of themselves as well. I almost lost my job.

They wanted to put me on medical retirement when I was 27 because I was in and out of the hospital a lot. But my work was at such a high level that they could not justify filing my medical retirement. I even went to them while on drugs, and they said I have a problem; I am on heroin. Then they sent me to rehab for five weeks. Two years later, I got promoted. God has been gracious. I should not have had a job; I never knew God heals mental disorders until 2021 when He healed me. I had been crying, and I said, "It's too hard to follow you. I can't measure up to the standards you have set me." I was at a very low point. After so many years of medications and hospitals, I was done. I was in the hospital 13 times.

My previous overdoses were not meant to kill me but to rest, to escape the sorrow, pain, and confusion of mental illness. I like to solve problems, and it was frustrating not to have a cure for it. All the therapy I had were only a band-aid. I was at the point where I was done. In September, I went to a national prophetic women's camp in South Africa at the invitation of a friend. I did not want to go to the camp, but my friend said I could co-lead worship with the pastor and with her. I liked that idea, so I went. Before the women came, I sought out a quiet spot.

I sat on a wooden bench and said to the Lord. "I am here to lead worship, but I am feeling like I don't want to do it anymore." I was crying out to him. All of a sudden, I said, "That is it! I'm going to hang myself. I think I've made a mistake, so I might as well get out of the way. I will do this camp well. I will do this well before I hang myself."

The women arrived. On the third and last night of the camp, the pastor said, "I feel like the Lord wants to minister to you tonight, so just go in the crowd with the women, and I will handle the worship." I said OK. At the end of the worship, the pastor's wife said "If you want prayers for anything, come up." And then they were bellowing a blue banner. The pastor's wife was standing under it. People went up to her, and as she prayed, people fell under the anointing of the Holy Spirit.

I heard the Holy Spirit say to me, "I want you to go up. Let her pray for you." I was helping others go for the prayer and was to sit. Then the pastor called me by my nickname, "Mixy! Please don't go. Come, let her pray for you." That was my Kairos moment. I looked at his wife, Rene, and started crying. It was like a sea of people made way for me to get to the front.

As I started walking, I felt this was it. God is going to do something. She looked at me as if she knew what I had told the Lord before the meeting. We both cried and spoke in tongues. She lifted my hands. It felt like a volcano at that moment, like everything inside wanted to explode. I told God I did not know what was happening. He told me to open my mouth, and I let out a scream, and then my knees got weak.

I dropped down and wept for two hours. I looked around and felt everything. It was as if I now had coloured lenses. With bipolar disorder, you don't have normal regulation of emotions, so they are switched off, especially with the medicine. That was the exact thing I was always crying out to God for; to have life inside of me. When I felt it, it was the most incredible feeling. I was free at last.

The Holy Spirit answered me and said, "I have healed you." I don't have kidney, liver, or stomach problems anymore. That was so incredible. I went home and said to God, "People have to know this." I don't want people to commit suicide. I learned that what cancer is to the body, is what bipolar is to the soul. I asked God last year, "How many times did I die?" He said, "It's not important, but I've saved you." I had an experience in a hospital where I heard the wail of the heart machine and saw myself on the bed.

At first, I thought I saw an angel in the room, too, but it was Jesus. I could not turn my head because of His glory. I felt so much love. When I looked at myself, I felt what He felt: I saw a precious, beautiful woman with no life. I heard Him say in my spirit, "Do you want this?" I said, "No, I want to live. I just do not want to be dead while I am alive". Last year, I saw a vision of what Jesus would do every time I would pass out when I tried to kill myself.

He would pick up my limp body, run to the Father, and scream and say, "No!" He would cry. He is so passionate. It's not His will for people to go through this. It hurts Him. I want to see people healed of mental illness and freed from suicidal thoughts. Thank you, Jesus, for healing me. I am so grateful, Father!

- MIXY JOHN

HEALED FROM CHRONIC COUGH

I had been experiencing a cough and difficulty swallowing for some time. I wasn't sure what was wrong, but I suspected it was something serious. I planned on going to the doctor on July 6th to get checked. I took a couple of days off work so I could come to Bethel and pray.

When I arrived on Friday, I went directly to the prayer house. The Lord told me to leave two minutes after I took communion, which surprised me. As I was leaving, an older woman with a walker was coming in. I stopped to talk to her, and she told me she was an intercessor. She shared that she had a healing ministry. I then asked her to pray for me, which she did.

Later that day, I had a sirloin steak and all the things that go with it from Outback Steakhouse. I had no coughing or symptoms in my throat afterwards as I'd had before. On Saturday morning, after breakfast, I didn't have any symptoms, either. I ran into the woman who prayed for me later, and she shared a great miracle she had seen on a mission trip to Cairo. That testimony boosted my faith even more. I was so happy that I got healed within half an hour of arriving at Bethel. I said, "God must have known I was coming." Thank you, Jesus!

- HOPE BENSON

HEALED FROM A LIFELONG AFFLICTION

On December 1, 2022, I went to our activation for healing and pastoral care. The leader, Roy, was talking about The Chosen, an episode in Season 3 where a disciple spoke to Jesus and wanted healing, and Jesus said He wanted to heal him but it would glorify Him more if he stayed with his infirmity. That was uncomfortable for me because I like The Chosen and did not want to criticize it, but that scene was disturbing to me, too.

As we discussed this in our class, we decided, "Let's pray the actor gets healed!" He has cerebral palsy, and we thought that maybe they wrote that in the script because of that. We said we did not want to change our theology according to our experience but model it to fit who God is. We prayed for that actor to be healed so they would have to change the storyline. We came to worship afterwards. I usually don't go to the front, but Payton (my friend) always does. That day, I was in front of her.

I turned around and said to her, "Healing is in your body!" Payton said, "Yeah!" She receives it so easily. I thought maybe I could be a little more intentional. I turned to her and said, "Hey, we talked about cerebral palsy this morning. And we prayed. Can I pray for you?" I had prayed for her before because she told me she had cerebral palsy. I lay my hands on her and prayed for realignment in her body and for every cell to vibrate at the frequency of heaven.

I asked her to test it out. To be honest, I was expectant and not expectant at the same time. She straightened and said, "Oh, my back just cracked." She held out her arms and said, "Are my arms the same length?" Her right arm was about an inch shorter than her left arm before. She started crying because she realized they were the same length. I started crying too.

I asked her to try out her legs, which would always hurt. I understood that, for her whole life, her foot spasmed every time she stretches it. It would hurt when she stands on it the whole day, and she would drag her foot a little behind her at the end of the day. She took her foot out of her slippers and stretched it out, but it did not spasm or hurt. She kept crying. I said, "You have to go up on stage and share!" The next day, I thought, "Is she still healed?" I was happy to have experienced this, but I wanted it to be permanent.

I texted her and asked if she was still healed, and she said, "Yes!" Her brain is now able to control her right side properly. I was so overwhelmed with joy and so honoured to be the one God used to heal her. All glory to Jesus!

- ROY JOHN

HEALED OF TRAUMATIC BRAIN INJURY

On June 1st, a Wednesday, G. had an accident and experienced blunt trauma from a fall, which lacerated the back of his head, and he sustained a traumatic brain injury. Combative and bleeding profusely, he was rushed to the hospital minutes after the incident.

A day or two later, he was awake and eating apple sauce. Soon after that, his brain began to swell, and a week after the accident, on a Wednesday, his brain was swelling so much that they did a craniectomy. A huge piece of his skull was removed to allow space for the swelling. At that point, he was being cared for in the trauma intensive care unit, on a ventilator with a feeding tube, and was monitored from head to toe.

The doctors did everything they could to reduce the swelling in his brain. He was non-responsive, and he would squeeze a hand when squeezed, but they did not know if he was hearing them. The doctors kept trying to get him to respond. They would yell, "G., wake up! G., can you hear me?" They would pinch him, take a bottle cap and push on the back of his cuticle to get him to respond to pain at the least.

By Thursday, there was a slight response; but by Friday, there was none. The palliative care team was involved, the family was advised, and medically, they could not do anything anymore to reduce the swelling. By this time, the area where the cranium was removed was now fuller and larger than when the skull was in place, rather than being sunken because of the missing structure. If the brain swells too much, it herniates, and the patient dies immediately.

That Friday evening, his wife, mom, and best friend met with the medical staff and palliative care unit. He had been specific about his wishes: he did not want to be resuscitated or live below his full capacity. Doctors said it was unusual that he had already planned this at the age of 36. He had also registered to be an organ donor. By evening, his family members were filling out the documentation for donor services.

They knew he wanted to bless someone else if possible, and it would honour him. He was healthy except for the trauma to his brain. They said their goodbyes that night and cried because the doctors did not know if he would make it through the night. If he did, the plan was that by Saturday evening, they would extubate him (he was dependent on the ventilator at that point).

They could be with him through the day, then go out while they extubate him, and he would die within minutes. Then they could go in to be with him while he transitioned to heaven. Once he was pronounced dead, the family would have two minutes with him. He would be rolled down the hall, celebrated with the "Walk of Honor," to the operating room, where teams of doctors would harvest his organs. Donor services asked if they would like to have a medallion of his fingerprint. His wife and mom said yes.

The next morning, his mom went to the hospital, and the nurse said, "Hey, G., look! Your mom's here." She looked at the nurse. The nurse said, "Show her how you can move your tongue." That meant his eyes were open, he was alert, he could understand speech, and he was responding to commands. The family was told he would most likely be blind because of the damage to his occipital lobe, but apparently, he wasn't!

Sometimes a patient would rally for a few days, and only time would tell. They celebrated and continued to pray. His mom said, "We stood in faith, with wild hope, knowing that God is good, God is faithful, and Jesus already bought and paid for our healing!" Things looked good for a couple of days. Then he started to decline.

By the middle of the following week, they had meetings with palliative care again, and by Friday, he had been moved to palliative care in another building. One can only be intubated for a certain number of days. He had reached the maximum. He had to be extubated. Sometime during the week, he had begun to breathe on his own, but the vent was still there and would push if he did not breathe. He was also receiving oxygen. They had never tried it without the ventilator.

His family had said no to a tracheotomy because they knew he would not have wanted to live the rest of his life with a tracheotomy. Doctors showed the CT scans and MRIs and explained the percentage of people who make it, the various levels of recovery, and the timeline of recovery, which could be years in a facility.

They said he had a 50% chance of recovering and being able to stay at home. He would probably always need supervision and not be able to work. There was a 1–2% chance that he would almost fully recover but not go back to his job. His mom said that was one of her most sinking moments. She, his wife, and best friend agreed: "We can't let him live like that; he would hate it." His DNR was explicit. All the while, they said, "God can still do the miracle. We are not saying he is dying. We are saying he doesn't want life support. So that Friday, he was to be extubated and his feeding tube removed because it was also on the DNR list of things he did not want.

They said their "goodbyes" again. The family left the room while they removed the tubes and machines. And he breathed. They returned to the room, and he breathed some more. The next day, he was still breathing. His mom said, "Are you waiting for him to starve to death?" The nurse said, "It could be more than a week because he is so healthy." On Sunday which was Father's Day, he was moved to hospice at a different facility. (He is the father of four sons, five and under.) It was his best friend's birthday, one of the children's birthdays, and their ninth wedding anniversary. In the hospice, he began to wake up, become more alert, and ask for a drink. They gave him water and asked if he wanted protein-infused, highly caloric milk. He wanted that.

He was hungry and could only eat pureed foods. They had to be careful that he did not choke or inhale food. He never did. He ate more and more and became more and more alert. He was watching a TV show he liked, and his wife asked who one of the characters was, and he knew. He began to think more clearly, process more, ask more questions, relate more, and carry conversations. His humour and broad vocabulary were poking through the fog and confusion. To their surprise, the thumbprint medallions were delivered a couple of weeks later. His mom considers it a testimony piece. She said, "I don't think many people have an organ donor thumbprint necklace if they are still looking their son in the eye." One night, when she was in hospice, a nurse came in to give him medications. G. said, "What is this, anyway?" He was interrogating the nurse and wanting to know what each medication did and how many milligrams it was.

He talked the nurse into letting him hold the pill cup. He did not have all his fine motor skills, but the nurse hung in there with him. He wanted to hold the syringe (used to give oral medications). He was holding the pill in one shaky hand and twirling the syringe in the other while asking questions. The nurse was patient, and G. got the information and took the medication. Later in the hallway, his mom asked the nurse, "How were you able going to have that conversation?" The nurse replied, "That was a miracle!" He had lost 30 pounds between the time of the accident and when he started to eat. A physical therapist who goes to their church offered to come and do an evaluation. She got him to sit up in bed and stand. This was at least a week into the two weeks he was in hospice.

The family brought in two other therapists who were able to submit their evaluation as they were advocating for rehabilitation for G. About 10 days into his second week in hospice, it was established that G. was no longer eligible for hospice because he was recovering rather than dying. This meant that they would start paying for his bed while trying to get him into rehabilitation. The social worker and his wife made some calls. She was told they could add rehab to their insurance policy. Another miracle! They would make it retroactive to June 1, and their premium would increase a little bit. Naturally, his wife agreed.

Hospice does not transfer patients out, except "out the back door" or to the hospital. There was no protocol to transfer him from hospice to a rehabilitation hospital. The family had to sign him out, meaning they are taking responsibility. They had to personally arrange medical transport to take him to rehab. He spent two weeks in hospice and then transferred to rehab on a Friday. He started his therapies on Monday and made progress daily. He had physical therapy, occupational therapy, and speech therapy. After one great week, he was feeling stronger.

Provoked by some frustration, he abruptly got out of bed and climbed over the rail, setting off an alarm. He was not as strong as he thought, he nearly fell but managed with some help, to land on a chair. The nurses rushed in. He had some sort of "episode." He needed to get tested, so he was transferred to the main hospital via 911. His agitation led to this incident. G. spent rough five days in the hospital, thirty-eight hours in the emergency department, and the balance on the neuro floor. He was transferred to the rehab hospital, where he will work hard to meet all the goals set before him by his therapist for two weeks before being discharged to go home.

The doctors, therapists, medical staff, and surgeons were amazing. The rehabilitation hospital team lined the walls of the hallway and celebrated G. as he walked out the doors upon his discharge. His mom said that standing by the bedside, praying, declaring, and reading scripture and handouts from the healing rooms helped her stay focused. She would play worship music. The presence of the Lord is real! G. had a blown-out eardrum from the accident, but he can hear now. His mom sent out updates, and many were praying. The prayer warriors were an encouragement and blessing. She commented about a couple of people saying something like, "We know he will be healed whether it is here or in heaven." She said, "I felt an alarm in my spirit at that comment, like never before."

"Although it's true and seems like a kind thing to say, do we say this because we are protecting hearts — ours or the person we are consoling? Are we already putting into place something that is going to make us feel better if we don't get what we are praying for? To me, this felt like a divided heart. That's what the Lord was teaching me. So, I decided not to go down that road of finding peace in either outcome. Leaning with absolute dependence on the faithfulness of God, not compromising what I was believing for. Knowing that if G. did not survive, God would care for my heart, I had to stay all in with wild hope!"

- WILL G

ABOUT THE AUTHOR

Roanna Baleta is a child of God who is passionate about preaching healing to the world. God said the world is sick and it is her duty as His daughter to spread his words of healing. She is a member of Living Faith Church. Aka. Winners Chapel. She is a great lover of God, living to please her heavenly father.

A student of the University of Benin, in her second year of study. "I Am The Lord, Your Healer" is her very first Christian book and it is born out of God's will to write a book about healing. As a child of God, she is fulfilling the will of her Father.